YEARNING FOR MORE

What Our Longings Tell Us
About God and Ourselves

BARRY MORROW

To Dinno—
I hope the book
creates a deep thirst
for Heaven!
Barry Morrow
I Cor. 15:19

IVP Books

An imprint of InterVarsity Press
Downers Grove, Illinois

InterVarsity Press
P.O. Box 1400, Downers Grove, IL 60515-1426
World Wide Web: www.ivpress.com
E-mail: email@ivpress.com

InterVarsity Press® is the book-publishing division of InterVarsity Christian Fellowship/USA®, a movement of students and faculty active on campus at hundreds of universities, colleges and schools of nursing in the United States of America, and a member movement of the International Fellowship of Evangelical Students. For information about local and regional activities, write Public Relations Dept., InterVarsity Christian Fellowship/USA, 6400 Schroeder Rd., P.O. Box 7895, Madison, WI 53707-7895, or visit the IVCF website at <www.intervarsity.org>.

While all stories in this book are true, some names and identifying information in this book have been changed to protect the privacy of the individuals involved.

Cover design: Cindy Kiple
Interior design: Beth Hagenberg
Images: © Judith Rosenbaum/NonStock/Getty Images

ISBN 978-0-8308-5636-7

Printed in the United States of America ∞

Library of Congress Cataloging-in-Publication Data has been requested.

P	18	17	16	15	14	13	12	11	10	9	8	7	6	5	4	3	2	1
Y	27	26	25	24	23	22	21	20	19	18	17	16	15	14	13	12

Contents

Foreword

As the deer pants for the water brooks,
So my soul pants for You, O God.
My soul thirsts for God, for the living God;
When shall I come and appear before God?

PSALM 42:1-2

Longing to see God and to enter his consummate presence is an oft-repeated theme in the writings of the great saints in the history of the church, but it is rarely seen in the Christian literature of our time. This is why I welcome the publication of *Yearning For More: What Our Longings Tell Us About Ourselves and God.* As you will discover, my friend Barry Morrow has a penchant for leveraging culture to illuminate timeless spiritual issues.

Moses' great prayer in the wilderness was "I pray You, show me Your glory!" (Exodus 33:18). The psalmists cultivated a passion for God's presence and understood that anything of true value comes from his hand. The sages who wrote the wisdom literature stressed that nothing at all can compare with knowing God. The prophets were overwhelmed with the splendor and majesty of God, and they endured ridicule and rejection in order to be pleasing to him. Jesus taught his followers to hunger and thirst more for God's kingdom and righteousness than for anything else. The apostles' deepest longing was to behold the infinite lover of their souls.

Six hundred years ago Julian of Norwich, in her *Revelations of Divine Love*, asked God for the three faithful wounds: contrition for her sins, compassion for others and an intense longing for God. "At the same moment," she wrote,

> the Trinity filled me full of heartfelt joy, and I knew that all eternity was like this for those who attain heaven. For the Trinity is God, and God the Trinity; the Trinity is our Maker and keeper, our eternal lover, joy and bliss—all through our Lord Jesus Christ. . . . We have got to realize the littleness of creation and to see it for the nothing that it is before we can love and possess God who is uncreated. This is the reason why we have no ease of heart or soul, for we are seeking our rest in trivial things which cannot satisfy, and not seeking to know God, almighty, all-wise, all-good. He is true rest. It is His will that we should know Him, and His pleasure that we should rest in Him. Nothing less will satisfy us. . . . We shall never cease wanting and longing until we possess Him in fullness and joy. Then we shall have no further wants. Meanwhile His will is that we go on knowing and loving until we are perfected in heaven. . . . The more clearly the soul sees the blessed face by grace and love, the more it longs to see it in its fullness.

C. S. Lewis in his autobiography, *Surprised by Joy*, related true joy to what he called *Sehnsucht*, or longing. In *The Weight of Glory* he spoke of the stab and pang of acute longing as homesickness for a place and a time we have not yet visited that is beyond the edge of the imagination.

> The sense that in this universe we are treated as strangers, the longing to be acknowledged, to meet with some response, to

bridge some chasm that yawns between us and reality, is part of our inconsolable secret. And surely, from this point of view, the promise of glory, in the sense described, becomes highly relevant to our deep desire. For glory meant good report with God, acceptance by God, response, acknowledgment, and welcome into the heart of things. The door on which we have been knocking all our lives will open at last. . . . Apparently, then, our lifelong nostalgia, our longing to be reunited with something in the universe from which we now feel cut off, to be on the inside of some door which we have always seen from the outside, is no mere neurotic fancy, but the truest index of our real situation. And to be at last summoned inside would be both glory and honour beyond all our merits and also the healing of that old ache.

There have been times when a walk in the woods, a painting, a photograph or a piece of music created a sudden and profound sense of longing within me. When I thought about it, I realized that in each case, the vehicle that caused the longing pointed not to itself but to that which is beyond the created order, to God himself. These are fleeting moments, but they are enough to remind me of the reality of my pilgrim status and to awaken desire for something more than anything this world can offer.

Along similar lines, Henri Nouwen in his perceptive book *The Return of the Prodigal Son* describes the remarkable effect Rembrandt's painting of this parable had on his self-understanding.

It had brought me into touch with something within me that lies far beyond the ups and downs of a busy life, something that represents the ongoing yearning of the human spirit, the yearning for a final return, an unambiguous sense of safety, a lasting home.

It is an aspiration to turn to our Father's house and to find the deep satisfaction of his embrace and of being treasured by him.

In My Father's house are many dwelling places; if it were not so, I would have told you; for I go to prepare a place for you. If I go and prepare a place for you, I will come again and receive you to Myself, that where I am, *there* you may be also. (John 14:2-3)

Coming to Christ is, as A. W. Tozer describes it in his *The Pursuit of God,*

not an end but an inception, for now begins the glorious pursuit, the heart's happy exploration of the infinite riches of the Godhead. That is where we begin, I say, but where we stop no man has yet discovered, for there is in the awful and mysterious depths of the Triune God neither limit nor end. . . . To have found God and still to pursue Him is the soul's paradox of love, scorned indeed by the too-easily-satisfied religionist, but justified in happy experience by the children of the burning heart.

This holy desire, this transcendent ambition, is captured in Jesus' penetrating words: "Seek first His kingdom and His righteousness, and all these things will be added to you" (Matthew 6:33). God waits to be wanted, but he must be wanted for himself and not for some lesser good he may provide. May we ask for the grace to long for the beatific vision, for the vision of God himself.

There will no longer be any curse; and the throne of God and of the Lamb will be in it, and His bond-servants will serve Him; *they will see His face*, and His name will be on their foreheads. (Revelation 22:3-4, emphasis added)

Kenneth Boa, Ph.D., D.Phil.
President, Reflections Ministries

Introduction

*You don't know quite what it is
you want, but it just fairly makes your
heart ache you want it so.*

MARK TWAIN

It seems to be a particularly human phenomenon that we are insatiably curious about this life, trying to make sense of the world we find ourselves inhabiting. We marvel at the universe, and we marvel at the beginning and end of our lives. Where did we come from? Where are we going? Is there any real purpose or significance to our lives? I believe it was Loren Eiseley who once said that humankind is the only cosmic orphan, the only one in the universe who asks, "Why?"

I must confess at the outset of our journey that I have always had a somewhat skeptical take on religious answers to ultimate questions. I should have been born in Missouri, the "show me" state. Nevertheless, my educational background in the natural sciences and my reading over the years, including many of the great classics, have always made me curious about the human condition. Issues that the sciences alone can't answer, I don't believe.

I once had a friend who was running from God. He was trying to figure out life on his own. So he bought copies of most of the works of fiction that make up the lists of great classics and began to read through them, trying to figure out life. His conclusion? Almost all of these deal in some way with *God*. The human condition cannot be adequately explained without some idea of God in the formula. Whether we believe in God or disbelieve, all of us have some sort of "theological" position—even the atheist or agnostic, who doubts God's existence.

So, what does it mean to be human? What do we make of life's ultimate questions? How do we make sense of it all? Is there a spiritual journey for us to consider, or is it all an accident? We *all* have a worldview of how we account for life—none of us is truly objective. We bring all kinds of presuppositions to life, and those can be distilled down to fundamentally either a material or a religious worldview.

C. S. Lewis, the Oxford don who rejected Christian theism until his early thirties, found a welcome audience in Great Britain for his radio broadcast talks over the BBC to a war-torn country, after his return to faith in orthodox Christianity. His twenty-five talks, given from 1941 to 1944, would later become the bestselling book that has influenced many, *Mere Christianity*.

His books sell millions of copies annually, and the Chronicles of Narnia, Lewis's take on an imaginary world that a group of children can occasionally enter through a wardrobe, has sold millions of copies. And a number of these books have made their way to the big screen. It is in the world of Narnia that our deepest desires and longings are touched on, evoking hopes for a better world than we experience in this present world.

But in *Mere Christianity*, Lewis suggests to us that there can be either a religious or material worldview. Either matter *or* God is eternal; both cannot be right. Our take on this fundamental question determines how we see our lives unfolding before us. So is life simply random chance, or is it in some way a sacred dance?

Similarly, Lewis's book *Mere Christianity*, written over sixty years ago, has much to say to our day amid the assault of the new atheists, who decry religious conviction as though those who embrace a belief in God have jettisoned their minds. I believe he was on to something. Lewis believed that the very things that matter most in life (and how we view our world) are better explained by embracing what could be called a sacramental view of life—that all of life is imbued with hints of another world that awaits us.

In his chapter titled "Hope" in *Mere Christianity*, Lewis suggests that it is very difficult for us to want heaven at all, except in so far as "heaven" means meeting our loved ones again who have died. And yet, if we are honest with ourselves and look into our hearts, we know that we want something badly, but something that *cannot* be had in this present world. All sorts of things give us the promise of delivering, but they all let us down.

We have only three options, he suggests. First, the "Fool's Way" is the path taken by a man or woman who goes throughout life seeking fulfillment from the latest or newest acquisition or experience, whether it is an expensive travel destination, another lover or another diversion. Yet he remains discontent, bored with life. *Disenchanted.*

The second option is what he calls the way of the "Disillusioned 'Sensible Man.'" This is the way of the man or woman who settles down and learns not to expect much from life, believing that the whole human experience was a concocted "moonshine" all along. Better, Lewis reasons, for this man or woman not to expect too much rather than to become *disenchanted* with the reality that life just doesn't deliver in the end.

No, there is a third way, Lewis concludes: "The Christian Way." Here he writes of what this present world was intended to do for us:

> The Christian says, "Creatures are not born with desires unless satisfaction for those desires exists. A baby feels hunger: well, there is such a thing as food. . . . Men feel sexual desire: well, there is such a thing as sex. If I find in myself a desire which no experience in this world can satisfy, the most probable explanation is that I was made for another world. . . . Probably earthly pleasures were never meant to satisfy it, but only to arouse it, to suggest the real thing."[1]

Here Lewis sets forth the fundamental idea that the longings and yearnings that we experience in this present world were never intended to satisfy us totally, but to awaken us to an even greater fulfillment and delight in a world to come.

So when we reflect on this fantastic world that we inhabit, we can either become disenchanted because it lets us down or instead conclude that we were "made for another world." Lewis's words become the touchstone theme of this book, that all of our lives point us to something more, that everything in our lives carries what Peter Berger calls a "signal of transcendence," of another world before us. We need not become disenchanted with this present world, but rather, explore what these deep longings intimate about another world before us.

Socrates once declared, "The unexamined life is not worth living." It is my hope that this volume will help you examine your life and hopefully come to the conclusion that I have come to, that life is not "a walking shadow, a poor player that struts and frets his hour upon the stage, and then is heard no more . . . a tale told by an idiot, full of sound and fury, signifying nothing," as Shakespeare declared in Macbeth.

No, our lives, through all our pains and pleasures, joys and delights, friendships and disappointments, work and play, point to another world for which we were created. We become disenchanted here, but we were made for another world that awaits us.

Won't you journey with me?

Looking for Answers, but Finding Only Questions

Everywhere the Apostle Paul went,
there was either riot or revival.
Everywhere I go, they want to serve tea.

FORMER ARCHBISHOP OF CANTERBURY

You need chaos in your soul to
give birth to a dancing star.

FRIEDRICH NIETZSCHE

In one of his most popular short stories, "Pigeon Feathers," novelist John Updike tells the story of a fourteen-year-old boy named David who has recently moved to his mother's birthplace in the small farm community of Firetown. David is a voracious reader curious about his Christian heritage. After reading H. G. Wells's account of Jesus as an obscure political agitator who was crucified and presumably died a few weeks later—only to have a religion founded after him—David begins to wonder whether or not Christianity is true. After he is visited by a horrid vision of his own death—a revelation amounting to extinction—he looks to his parents to provide answers, but they are no help.

David then turns to his pastor, Reverend Dobson, a sophisticated and enlightened preacher and a bit misplaced in Firetown, who teaches a catechism class to the young people on Sunday afternoons. When the time comes for questions, David asks about the resurrection of the body and about whether we are conscious between the time we die and the Day of Judgment. "What will heaven be like?" David asks Reverend Dobson.

When Dobson suggests to David that heaven might be best understood as "the goodness Abraham Lincoln did living on after him," David feels betrayed. The only thing David wants is to hear Reverend Dobson repeat the words about the Christian hope of immortality that he said every Sunday morning. But David leaves that afternoon with a sense of indignation, not only at being betrayed, but of seeing Christianity betrayed. When he returns home and sits down with his grandfather's Bible, attempting to read it, his mother joins him on the sofa to see what is troubling him.

"I asked Reverend Dobson about Heaven and he said it was like Abraham Lincoln's goodness living after him."

"And why didn't you like it?"

"Well, don't you see? It amounts to saying there isn't any Heaven at all."

"I don't see that it amounts to that. What do you want Heaven to be?"

"Well, I don't know. I want it to be something. I thought he'd tell me what it was."

"David," she asked gently, "don't you ever want to rest?"

"No. Not forever."

"David . . . when you get older, you'll feel differently."

"Grandpa didn't. Look how tattered this book is."

"I think Reverend Dobson made a mistake. You must try to forgive him."

"It's not a question of his making a mistake! It's a question of dying and never moving or seeing or hearing anything ever again."

"But"—in exasperation—"darling, it's so greedy of you to want more. When God has given us this wonderful April day, and given us this farm, and you have your whole life ahead of you—"

"Mother . . . don't you see . . . if when we die there's nothing, all your sun and fields and what not are, ah, horror? It's just an ocean of horror."[1]

Few stories better capture the modern-day sentiment of our culture's belief—or disbelief—in the afterlife than Updike's "Pigeon Feathers." While many, like David's mother, have a wistful, ethereal idea about the afterlife, it's not saying too much to suggest that our culture at large has lost its sense of transcendence. But for many of us, like David, if we listen to our hearts, we want more than wonderful April days, beautiful vistas and all that *this* life can offer. Our souls cry out that our lives have an ultimate meaning and purpose that *transcends* this temporal life.

Looking for Meaning and Happiness in Religion

Many turn to organized faith and religion to fill the void in their lives, in the hopes of a better world to come. And while many have found meaning and fulfillment in their lives through their faith, contemporary culture at large has not been very kind to religious people, especially conservative Christians. In his book *Lost in the Cosmos: The Last Self-Help Book*, novelist

Walker Percy pokes fun at fundamentalist Christians when he playfully promises to inform his readership, "How you can survive in the Cosmos about which you know more and more while knowing less and less about yourself, this despite 10,000 self-help books, 100,000 psychotherapists, and 100 million fundamentalist Christians."[2]

While Percy embraced a spiritual worldview late in life, he was never comfortable in the conservative fundamentalist camp of Christendom. He once lamented that the Christian novelist is like a person who has found a "treasure hidden in the attic of an old house." Yet he concluded that he was writing for people who had "moved out to the suburbs" and who were "sick of the old house of orthodoxy" and everything in it.

But if we can't find purpose and meaning in religion, we find ourselves looking to other avenues in life to bring about a sense of purpose and meaning. Truth be known, we humans are a curious and restless bunch, always looking to the world to make us happy. And with the frenetic pace of modern life amid e-mails, twittering, streaming media and jammed work and personal lives, we complicate our lives with busyness, believing that this will deliver to us the happiness that we so desperately desire.

A Restless Culture in Search of Happiness

Ours is a restless culture in a quest for happiness, a culture in pursuit of the Good Life. And how do we seek happiness? Deeply embedded in our minds is the fundamental belief that acquiring more things, bigger and better things, will ultimately make us happy. We run ourselves ragged looking for the next great experience, vacation or diversion in life, thinking that these will bring solace to our souls.

The story is told of a young author who was writing a book

about the people of Appalachia. As he traveled through a mountain valley, he noticed a large old house with an elderly, cigar-smoking man rocking on the front porch. He thought to himself, *I ought to interview this old man to see what keeps him going.* He sat down by the old man and inquired, "Tell me, you men of Appalachia live to be so old. What's the secret?"

The man responded, "It's no secret to me. I drink a quart of homemade whiskey every day, I smoke at least a half-dozen cigars like these every day, and I chase women at night."

With a look of astonishment, the young writer replied, "That's incredible! Just how old are you?" With calmness in his voice, Gramps said, "I'll be thirty-two this October."

While most of us don't live like this man from Appalachia, many of us lament the frantic pace of contemporary life. In pursuit of happiness, we find ourselves performing the ultimate juggling act with work, family and leisure time. A new term has even been coined for multitasking: *time-stacking.* Time stackers are busy people who juggle two or more tasks at once, a behavior that has become rampant, especially among professionals.

Most of us have this right of entitlement, believing that we deserve all that life can possibly offer. Musing on this American mindset, Daniel Boorstin suggests that Americans suffer from all-too-extravagant expectations. In his much-quoted book, *The Image: A Guide to Pseudo-Events in America,* Boorstin makes this observation of Americans:

> We expect anything and everything. We expect the contradictory and the impossible. We expect compact cars which are spacious; luxurious cars which are economical. We expect to be rich and charitable, powerful and merciful, active and reflective, kind and competitive. . . . We expect

to eat and stay thin, to be constantly on the move and ever more neighborly, to go to a "church of our choice" and yet feel its guiding power over us, to revere God and to be God. Never have people been more the masters of their environment. Yet never has a people felt more deceived and disappointed. For never has a people expected so much more than the world could offer.[3]

Is That All There Is?

But even when we drink from the wellspring of advertising and accumulate goods with the hopes of self-fulfillment, more often than not we are greeted with a certain disillusionment and emptiness.

The lesson is clear. Despite our accumulation of things, Americans still find ourselves yearning for connectedness, simplicity and meaning. For all the trumped-up promises of happiness and fulfillment from our achievements, acquisitions and accomplishments, if we are honest with ourselves, we will admit that they often leave us frazzled and disillusioned. Years ago the country singer Peggy Lee recorded a hit song titled "Is That All There Is?" Many of us have found ourselves asking that question. All of this leads to the fundamental question that sooner or later we have to confront. That question is this: *Can this world really make us happy?*

Many people today have reached the pinnacle of personal, financial and career success, despite the unprecedented economic tsunami of the past few years. Still, they have what some have called "destination sickness." They have arrived, but they are sick and disillusioned. They may have all the outward appearances of success, but deep inside they are hollow and empty. They are perhaps hungry for things beyond this world, because this world alone cannot sustain a lasting happiness.

Jon Katz, a former executive producer with CBS, has gone on record describing his own spiritual odyssey and search amid personal success in his book *Running to the Mountain: A Journey of Faith and Change*. Katz describes his own quest, when "bread and circuses" had let him down:

> Ten years earlier, as executive producer of the two-hour program *The CBS Morning News*, I had stood in a control room one day before dawn, staring at a wall of high-tech color monitors. The co-anchor of the spectacularly unsuccessful show I produced, a former beauty queen and sports commentator named Phyllis George, was smiling back at me surreally from all of them. An assistant dabbed at her make-up and fluffed her hair. I was powerful, well-compensated, lost. A few minutes later, I was locked in my office, weeping. I had reached a rung in my life a lot of people would have coveted, and I would rather have thrown myself off a bridge than stay there for another month. So, tentatively, with equal parts of determination and terror, I set off on what Thomas Merton liked to call a journey of the soul.[4]

Katz came to the important realization that one can have all this world has to offer and still be miserable on the inside. He, like many an "up-and-outer" (the opposite of a "down-and-outer"), had reached the pinnacle of success by the standards of the world, yet he was despairing. He came to the conclusion that the true journey of life is a spiritual journey, a journey of the soul.

Were We Meant to Be Happy?

Peggy Noonan, a former presidential speechwriter and frequent contributor to the *Wall Street Journal*, raises an important question in her book *What I Saw at the Revolution*, when she asks, were we made to be happy here? Noonan suggests that much of our unhappiness is born out of a huge cultural revolution within the baby boomer generation. The salient feature of this revolution, Noonan contends, is the *expectation* of happiness. She writes,

> It is 1956 in the suburbs, in the summer. A man comes home from work, parks the car, slouches up the driveway. His white shirt clings softly to his back. He bends for the paper, surveys the lawn, waves to a neighbor. From the house comes his son, freckled, ten. He jumps on his father; they twirl on the lawn. Another day done. Now water the lawn, eat fish cakes, watch some TV, go to bed, do it all again tomorrow.
>
> Is he happy? No. Why should he be? We weren't put here to be happy. But the knowledge of his unhappiness does not gnaw. Everyone is unhappy, or rather everyone has a boring job, a marriage that's turned to disinterest, a life that's turned to sameness. And because he does not expect to be happy the knowledge of his unhappiness does not weigh on him. He looks perhaps to other, more eternal forms of comfort.[5]

In a similar fashion, the French philosopher and mathematician Blaise Pascal perhaps put his finger on the problem some three hundred and fifty years ago. In his famous *Pensées* ("meditations"), he contended that we seek diversions in life to assuage our unhappiness: "If our condition were truly happy we should not need to divert ourselves from thinking about it. . . . That is why we prefer the hunt to the capture. That is why men are so fond of hustle and bustle."

These *pensées* are arguably the most powerful and relevant for our modern culture, which ironically has more leisure than our ancestors ever experienced. Despite all of our labor-saving devices, we are still a society that is largely discontent. Pascal's words even suggest that the society that has the most diversions and amusements is in fact the unhappiest.

And this accurately describes our dilemma. We run around, harried, hassled and complaining that we never have enough time—though we really don't want to simplify our lives. In reality, we want the very thing we complain about. We gripe about not having enough leisure time to kick back, reflect and unwind. Yet for many of us, more time for leisure and reflection would be unbearable. Why? We seek to be diverted from thinking about transcendent things. They are too threatening to us. We crave *diversions* to keep us from genuine solitude.

Philosopher Peter Kreeft believes that our fear of solitude may even suggest a deeper fear of our mortality. He writes,

> If you are typically modern, your life is like a rich mansion with a terrifying hole right in the middle of the living-room floor. So you paper over the hole with a very busy wallpaper pattern to distract yourself. You find a rhinoceros in the middle of your house. The rhinoceros is wretchedness and death. How in the world can you hide a rhinoceros? Easy: cover it with a million mice. Multiply diversions.[6]

A number of years ago, we were greeted with the revealing slogan emblazoned on car bumpers and T-shirts: "He who dies with the most toys wins." In a society that has lost its sense of purpose and meaning, banality becomes the prevalent notion of the day. And our culture of amusement and entertainment bears eloquent testimony that we are generally an unhappy and unsatisfied people who seek to anesthetize our unhappiness with busyness and diversions. And if life really felt like a holiday, we wouldn't be so driven to take holidays from it.

What Lies Behind Our Unhappiness?

In this troubled, unhappy world of ours, it is typically the artist who, because he or she lives on the cutting edge of culture, reflects with deep honesty the true sentiment of the age. Walker Percy, whose novel *The Moviegoer* was nominated for the National Book Award, was a remarkable diagnostician of the soul. An artist of sorts and a philosopher, he once wrote about the prophetic role of the novelist, in what he calls a certain *upsidedownness* in modern life. Percy makes this insightful remark about the role of the artist-novelist in his essay "Novel-Writing in an Apocalyptic Time":

> If the novelist's business is, like that of all artists, to tell the truth . . . he had better tell the truth no matter how odd it is, even if the truth is a kind of upsidedownness. . . . Whenever you have a hundred thousand psychotherapists talking about being life-affirming and a million books about life-enrichment, you can be sure there is a lot of death around. . . . Could it be that this paradoxical diminishment of life in the midst of plenty, its impoverishment in the face of riches, is the peculiar vocation of the novelist. . . . There is something worse than being deprived of life: it is being deprived of life and not knowing it. The poet and the novelist cannot bestow life but they can point to instances of its loss.[7]

Percy's words speak powerfully to the malaise that is so pervasive in our contemporary culture.

Many would argue that this world cannot provide us with a lasting happiness. Indeed, I would submit that the loneliest times in our lives occur when what we believe will deliver the ultimate satisfaction is experienced, and we are still let down. This bitter irony meets us not so much in our disappointments, but more often amid our joys and happiness. It seems that when life treats us best, the deepest dissatisfaction arises in our souls.

So, what is it that Peggy Noonan, Jon Katz, Walker Percy and others are calling us to? Could it be that they want us to explore the deep root of our lack of satisfaction and happiness with this world? Could it be that part of the answer is the realization that our happiness lies not in "bread and circuses," but in something else, beyond this world, more lasting and enduring?

There was a time in my life when I truly believed that a beautiful sports car or an exotic travel vacation (both of which I enjoy) would bring me lasting happiness. But they have not done so.

What are the things of this world that you and I have set our affections on to bring us happiness? Is it people? A new job or car? A dream holiday away from the hustle and bustle, a second or third home? Have you and I come to the point in our lives where we know there is no lasting happiness, no material possessions, no extraordinary experiences, no significant achievements that will ultimately satisfy us? Have we come to the place where we know that everything under the sun, so to speak, has a built-in fizzle to it?

Perhaps this is the first step in the journey. Maybe we are disenchanted with this present world because we were made for *another* world.

-2-

Seeking Happiness

Advice from an Ancient Sage

There are two tragedies in life.
One is not getting what you want.
The other is getting it.

OSCAR WILDE

Man finds it hard to
get what he wants, because he does
not want the best; God finds it hard to give,
because He would give the best, and
man will not take it.

GEORGE MACDONALD

In the first chapter we observed how, try as we may to find contentment and happiness in this world, we are still left disenchanted. It seems that in this temporal world, our lives are filled with yearning, seeking and trying to find a lasting peace and happiness when none is there. And if we are honest with ourselves, we will admit that it seems that even in our times of greatest joy and happiness, that emptiness remains in our souls, and we wonder why we are still left so empty.

One of the amazing things about the unsettled happiness that is so predominant in our modern Western culture is that it has been a part of the fabric of the human condition from time immemorial. One of the most interesting records we have of this striving for happiness, meaning and purpose is found in an unlikely place, written three millennia ago, by none other than Solomon, sometimes referred to as Qoheleth, the ancient king of Israel.

While there is much that could be said about Solomon, reputed to be one of the wisest sages of the ancient world, the chronicling of his life experiences in the pursuit of happiness in the ancient book of Ecclesiastes is one of the most respected and admired of any in the world. And this is irrespective of one's religious persuasion. The great American novelist Thomas Wolfe once said of Ecclesiastes,

> Of all that I have ever seen or learned, [the biblical book of Ecclesiastes] seems to me the noblest, the wisest, and the most powerful expression of man's life upon this earth, and also the highest flower of poetry, eloquence and truth. . . . Ecclesiastes is the greatest single piece of writing I have ever known, and the wisdom expressed in it the most lasting and profound.[1]

Few works so vividly portray such a remarkable attempt to create a secular Utopia than Solomon's account in Ecclesiastes. Having almost a timeless and prophetic nature, it speaks powerfully to our twenty-first-century culture. Great literary minds have long admired this seemingly pessimistic but timeless tome on life. The God-haunted agnostic Herman Melville once declared in *Moby Dick* that "the truest of all books is

Ecclesiastes." Commenting on the uniqueness of the book, British writer Derek Kidner observes,

> Anyone who spends time with Ecclesiastes (that least ecclesiastical of men) finds himself in the company of a highly independent and fascinating mind. . . . But there is no-one quite like Qoheleth (to give him his untranslatable title); no book in this whole great volume speaks in quite his tone of voice. His natural habitat, so to speak, is among the wise men who teach us to use our eyes as well as our ears to learn the ways of God and man. . . . Wisdom—quite practical and orthodox—is his base-camp; but he is an explorer. His concern is with the boundaries of life, and especially with the questions that most of us would hesitate to push too far.[2]

Despite the prophetic wisdom contained in Ecclesiastes, because the Preacher pushes the boundaries of life, the book is often regarded as a classic work of despair, cynicism and ambiguity. Let's look briefly at this idea of ambiguity in Ecclesiastes.

The Ambiguity of Ecclesiastes

While the idea of ambiguity and uncertainty may not sit well with many of us, especially those of a religious persuasion, a strong sense of ambiguity and cynicism is part of the prevalent mood of our culture at large. Many have observed a certain cynicism that pervades life.

- Alexander Pope once declared, "Blessed is he who expects nothing, for he shall never be disappointed."

- Lily Tomlin mused, "Things are going to get a lot worse before they get worse."

- Woody Allen observed, "Life is divided into the horrible and the miserable."

- James Hagerty declared, "One day I sat thinking almost in despair; a hand fell on my shoulder and a voice said reassuringly: 'Cheer up, things could get worse.' So I cheered up and, sure enough, things got worse."

- George Burns made the witty observation, "Happiness is having a large, loving, caring, close-knit family . . . in another city."

A primary reason for Solomon's cynicism is that life presents us with many ambiguities. And this is where the rub comes with a lot of religious people with Solomon's words, as it is sometimes assumed that the Good Life will always be the reward for faithfulness to God. This kind of prosperity theology promises blessings, riches and a life of comfort if we will only "give our lives to Jesus" and become his devoted followers. Such thinking goes along the lines of "God has a wonderful plan for your life."

But Solomon shows us that this present life is greatly characterized by ambiguity and does not necessarily reward the righteous or punish the guilty. He observes in Ecclesiastes 8:14: "There is futility which is done on the earth, that is, there are righteous men to whom it happens according to the deeds of the wicked. On the other hand, there are evil men to whom it happens according to the deeds of the righteous. I say that this too is futility."

Eugene Peterson speaks about life's ambiguity in his book *Run with the Horses:*

> Flannery O'Connor once remarked that she had an aunt who thought that nothing happened in a story unless somebody got married or shot at the end of it. But the truth of the matter is that life seldom provides such definitive endings. Life is ambiguous. There are loose ends. It takes maturity to live with the ambiguity and the chaos, the absurdity and the untidiness. If we refuse to live with

it, we exclude something, and what we exclude may very well be the essential and dear—the hazards of faith, the mysteries of God.[3]

And if we are honest with ourselves, whether we have a religious orientation about life or not, we will admit that life often is dumfounding to us. If we don't see the ambiguity in the questions of life, we will be sorely disappointed.

The Modernity of Ecclesiastes

It is no mistake to see that modern day life is lived by many people without a kind of religious frame of reference. While the religious faithful gather at their houses of worship on Sunday mornings, many more can be found at their parks for a morning run, on a bike ride or reading the *New York Times* over coffee at their local Starbucks.

In many respects, the world has "come of age," to use Dietrich Bonhoeffer's phrase, and no longer considers some idea of God as necessary to account for humankind and the world. And yet we find this three-thousand-year-old book in the Old Testament of the Bible, and it seems as modern as tomorrow's newspaper.

Solomon, the Preacher, sets forth a brutally honest appraisal of life. The writer Robert Short authored the curious *A Time to Live and a Time to Die*, which is a book of contemporary photographs, one for each verse of Ecclesiastes. In a similar fashion, we might best understand Ecclesiastes as a series of word photographs or "light writings," pictures taken with available light "under the sun" (a key phrase that occurs twenty-nine times in Ecclesiastes).

For unlike the other biblical writers, Qoheleth informs us about life by using only the available light "under the sun": observation and human reason. He or she has no flashbulb of faith to illuminate life's ambiguities.

Because the Preacher is using only natural revelation, without the aid of faith, the book is inviting us not so much to think as to *feel*. Ecclesiastes is an existential book. Does my existence have any meaning? While earlier ages debated what the meaning of human existence was, our day asks the more fundamental question, *is* there meaning in our existence? If there is one fate for all, namely death, can anything have significance? If every card in our hand will be trumped, does it really matter how we play?

Listen to Qoheleth's lament:

> For there is no lasting remembrance of the wise man as with the fool, inasmuch as in the coming days all will be forgotten. And how the wise man and the fool alike die! So I hated life, for the work which had been done under the sun was grievous to me. . . . Thus I hated all the fruit of my labor for which I had labored under the sun, for I must leave it to the man who will come after me. (Ecclesiastes 2:16-18)

Here we have Solomon assaulting perhaps our greatest fear, which is not so much the fear of death (ancient man's deepest fear) but the fear of meaninglessness. Throughout the book, Qoheleth uses the word *vanity* (Hebrew *hevel*) thirty-five times to stress the fact that all of life is vanity, ephemeral, transient, purposeless. But in Ecclesiastes, the word no longer means simply what is slight and passing, but more ominously, what is pointless. It is a *desperate* word.

There is an old movie, *Holiday*, that wonderfully captures the unsettledness of contemporary culture in its quest for meaning and purpose. These lines spoken by Cary Grant to Katherine Hepburn sound like a modern-day Solomon:

> Linda: How does your garden grow, Case? Is life wonderful where you are?

Johnny: It can be.

Linda: But it hasn't been?

Johnny: Well, I don't call what I've been doing living.

Linda: And what do you recommend for yourself, Doctor?

Johnny: A holiday.

Linda: For how long?

Johnny: As long as I need.

Linda: Just to play?

Johnny: No, no. I've been working since I was ten. I want to find out why I'm working. The answer can't be just to pay bills and to pile up more money. Even if you do, the government's going to take most of it.

Linda: Yes, but what is the answer?

Johnny: Well, I don't know. That's what I intend to find out.

The Strategy of Ecclesiastes

The strategy Solomon uses in getting us to consider the purpose and meaning of life is in keeping with the general air of cynicism that pervades the book. In many ways, he is seeking to knock the props out from under our lives—such props as money, fame and fortune—to get us to look at life from a new perspective. Peter Kreeft accurately describes his strategy:

> We also see his strategy within the disconcerting structure of Ecclesiastes. The book clearly defies any logical outline. It seems to ramble, going nowhere in particular, containing bits of wisdom here and there sprinkled over a desert landscape of futility and meaninglessness. It is kind of like a

collage of photos taken through the porthole of a sinking ship, yet this rambling is deliberate, for this form ideally suits the book's content. Just as life rambles, going nowhere (from a naturalistic, horizontal perspective), so Ecclesiastes practices what it preaches.[4]

In addition to the key words *vanity* and *under the sun*, which stress desperation, the phrase *what does man gain?* strongly supports Solomon's contention that life, for all its success, is in the end *undone*. It doesn't deliver. We become disenchanted. A free translation of this verse might read, "You spend your life working, laboring, and what do you have to show for it?" When one samples all that this life has to offer and still lacks happiness and fulfillment, and is disenchanted, where is one to turn? In a covert manner, the Preacher is exposing the bankruptcy of the world in its ability to provide ultimate meaning and purpose to life.

Five Candidates for the Greatest Good

But the Preacher is no ordinary teacher. He invites us on a journey that he himself has taken to see if any candidate under the sun can provide lasting happiness and fulfillment. At least five candidates, five efforts, five "toils," are introduced throughout the book. These are perhaps the five most universal approaches that we humans follow to find meaning and significance in life: wisdom, pleasure, power and riches, altruism and naturalistic religion.

Wisdom. The first of these candidates is philosophical intellectualism, or the pursuit of wisdom. Solomon desperately wants to know what the ultimate purpose of life is. He is a philosopher at heart, a lover of wisdom, so he naturally hopes that wisdom will provide this fulfillment.

I, the Preacher, have been king over Israel in Jerusalem. And I set my mind to seek and explore by wisdom concerning all that has been done under heaven. . . . I said to myself, "Behold, I have magnified and increased wisdom more than all who were over Jerusalem before me; and my mind has observed a wealth of wisdom and knowledge." And I set my mind to know wisdom and to know madness and folly; I realized that this also is striving after wind. Because in much wisdom there is much grief, and increasing knowledge results in increasing pain. (Ecclesiastes 1:12-13, 16-18)

Solomon's discovery bears an uncanny similarity to those in our own day, when we are unrivaled in our ability to discover, learn and access information about virtually anything under the sun. We can search on Google or Wikipedia with our iPhones or iPads and find virtually any data we want in a matter of seconds. Yet we come to realize the futility of looking to wisdom and information as if it will bring us lasting meaning and purpose.

How often have we, or others we know, sought knowledge and wisdom, advanced degrees and learning, as if all our knowledge, learning and credentials would answer the fundamental questions of meaning and human existence?

T. S. Eliot, the celebrated poet and literary critic, expresses this sentiment in his "Choruses from 'The Rock,'" when he declares that our knowledge leads us only to our "ignorance" and our ignorance "nearer to death," not God. Eliot then asks us to consider, "Where is the wisdom we have lost in knowledge?"

Pleasure. If happiness cannot be found through stimulating the mind (wisdom), then perhaps bodily pleasures will work (hedonism). Solomon's experiment with pleasure involved a virtual sensory overload, including wine, women and song. He experienced an almost utopian lifestyle. Listen to how he describes it:

> I said to myself, "Come now, I will test you with pleasure. So enjoy yourself." And behold, it too was futility. I said of laughter, "It is madness," and of pleasure, "What does it accomplish?" I explored with my mind how to stimulate my body with wine. . . . I enlarged my works: I built houses for myself, I planted vineyards for myself; I made gardens and parks for myself, and I planted in them all kinds of fruit trees; I made ponds of water for myself from which to irrigate a forest of growing trees. I bought male and female slaves. . . . Also I possessed flocks and herds larger than all who preceded me in Jerusalem. Also, I collected for myself silver and gold, and the treasure of kings and provinces. I provided for myself male and female singers and the pleasures of men—many concubines. . . . Thus I considered all my activities which my hands had done and the labor which I had exerted, and behold all was vanity and striving after wind and there was no profit under the sun. (Ecclesiastes 2:1-8, 11)

Just as our world is rampant in the quest for wisdom and information, the quest for pleasure as the purpose in life also holds a prominent place in our culture. In a world devoid of any eternal, transcendent dimension, the "pleasure principle" rules supreme.

I am reminded of Rousseau's comment that "happiness is a good bank account, a good cook, and good digestion." Or as the late comedian George Burns once put his own inimitable twist on the quote: "Happiness is a good meal, a good cigar, and a good woman. Or a bad woman, depending on how much happiness you can stand."

Because our world has become anesthetized to the spiritual world, our present temporal world is largely seen as our haven of rest. Consequently, the measure of life is to be found largely through the pleasures of this life. In Carnegie Hall's concert program a number of years ago, an advertisement selling luxury apartments captured today's *zeitgeist*: "Nobody gets out of life alive. So it makes superb common sense to live as beautifully, as comfortably, and as creatively as possible while one has the time. Life is too short to settle for second best."

Can't we each look at our own lives and think about the times that we have tried to escape reality through pleasure? All of us have sought happiness through a vacation, a new car, a trip to New York City or Europe, because deep down we believe these things will deliver, and make us happy. T. S. Eliot once observed that "humankind cannot bear very much reality," and so it is with us.

To those of us who probably do not "have it all," pleasures promise to fill the empty void, to bring happiness. Yet the truth of the matter is that we, like Solomon, become disillusioned with hedonistic aspirations. Why? Because in the end we sense that even pleasures are "vanity and striving after wind," because pleasure seeking inevitably produces boredom, apathy and disenchantment. And to overcome the inertia of boredom and apathy, we must experience even stronger doses of pleasure. There is a paradox to hedonism: the more we hunt for pleasure, the less we are able to find and sustain it.

Power and riches. If Solomon cannot find happiness from filling his mind with wisdom (intellectualism) or his body with pleasure (hedonism), then perhaps filling his wallet with money (materialism) is the answer. In his world as in ours, if we have wealth and power, we can buy the pleasures we desire.

A museum in Deadwood, South Dakota, illustrates this

beautifully. It displays artifacts from the Wild West era, and on one such display is a note left by an unsuccessfully successful prospector:

I lost my gun.
I lost my horse.
I am out of food.
The Indians are after me.
But I've got all the gold I can carry.

We may be carrying as much gold around as is humanly possible, so to speak, as we try to ignore the Indians. Similarly, it was Solomon's goal in life to amass great wealth at any expense: "Also, I collected . . . silver and gold, and the treasure of kings and provinces. . . . Then I became great and increased more than all who preceded me in Jerusalem" (Ecclesiastes 2:8-9).

We are amused at the folly of chasing wealth, but deep down we know that it describes us. And yet wealth leaves us disenchanted. Notable people through history have reminded us of the truth of wealth's failure to satisfy.

- John D. Rockefeller declared, "I have made many millions, but they have brought me no happiness."

- John Jacob Astor left five million dollars to his heirs, but at the end of his life lamented, "I am the most miserable man on earth."

- Andrew Carnegie once commented, no doubt from personal experience, "Millionaires seldom smile."

So Solomon here reminds us that fame and fortune do not bring ultimate happiness. Again, if we are honest with ourselves, when we think of the most satisfied times in our lives, they were times characterized by contentment with what we had in life. Listen to this conversation years ago between Jed Clampett and

Cousin Pearl in the television program *The Beverly Hillbillies*:

> Jed: Pearl, what d'ya think? Think I oughta move?
>
> Cousin Pearl: Jed, how can ya even ask? Look around ya. You're eight miles from yore nearest neighbor. Yore overrun with skunks, possums, coyotes, bobcats. You use kerosene lamps fer light and you cook on a wood stove summer and winter. Yore drinkin' homemade moonshine and washin' with homemade lye soap. And yore bathroom is fifty feet from the house and you ask "Should I move?"
>
> Jed: I reckon yore right. A man'd be a dang fool to leave all this!

Like the paradox of hedonism, there is a paradox of materialism. The more we look for happiness through wealth and power, the more disillusioned we become. Only the hunger remains. No, we need something more substantial than toys and trinkets to make this life meaningful.

John Steinbeck was on to something in his book *East of Eden*, when he declared, "Money is easy to make if it's money you want. But with few exceptions people don't want money. They want luxury and they want love and they want admiration."

Altruism. So Solomon reasons that if the key to life is not to be found in the selfish pursuit of filling his mind, body or pocketbook, perhaps it lies in service to others. This is his possible candidate for ultimate meaning and purpose, *altruism*. Perhaps through philanthropy and living for others—especially for posterity— life can have lasting significance, we reason. Yet as noble as this may seem, it is not enough to overcome a life of vanity:

> Thus I hated all the fruit of my labor for which I had labored under the sun, for I must leave it to the man who will come after me. And who knows whether he will be a

wise man or a fool? Yet he will have control over all the fruit of my labor for which I have labored by acting wisely under the sun. This too is vanity. (Ecclesiastes 2:18-19)

Solomon has come to the stark realization that it is meaningless to work for posterity because posterity may very well be a fool. How often have we seen men and women working all their lives to build up a great amount of net worth and then face the realization that their heirs will not be good stewards of the wealth that has been passed down to them? What exactly *is* the good of others? Don't we need to be asking that question today?

Naturalistic religion. As we return to Ecclesiastes, we hear Solomon reasoning, if intellectualism, hedonism, materialism and altruism prove unsatisfactory in providing ultimate purpose and meaning to life, perhaps religion will work. Conventional, naturalistic religion is Solomon's fifth candidate for purpose and meaning. His God is the God of reason and human experience, and his beliefs stem from sensory observation and human reason—"photographs" of life taken with the only available light "under the sun." Consider his sobering words:

Consider the work of God, for who is able to straighten what He has bent? In the day of prosperity be happy, but in the day of adversity consider—God has made the one as well as the other so that man may not discover anything that will be after him. I have seen everything during my lifetime of futility; there is a righteous man who perishes in his righteousness, and there is a wicked man who prolongs his life in his wickedness. Do not be excessively righteous and do not be overly wise. Why should you ruin yourself? Do not be excessively wicked and do not be a fool. Why should you die before your time? (Ecclesiastes 7:13-17)

One thing is certain about Qoheleth's musings on religion: he or she is a brutally honest observer. Irrespective of one's religious beliefs, or lack thereof, it is true to say that we live on a blighted planet where living a good life, a life with integrity, is not always rewarded with a long and happy life. Haven't you and I known good, faithful, religious people who have worked long and hard all their lives, just to have their lives snuffed out as they were about to enjoy the fruit of their years of labor?

So Solomon now comes to the end of his experiment, a disenchanted but wiser man. He may fill his mind with wisdom, his body with pleasure, his pockets with wealth, his conscience with good works or his spirit with religion, but in the end all his striving and accomplishments are *futile*. Man must look for something greater to bring lasting meaning and satisfaction.

He reminds me of Pascal's wise statement, "Anyone who does not see the vanity of life is vain indeed." And we, like Solomon, must often come to our wits' end to realize the futility of all our striving.

The End of the Journey

As the Preacher discovers, all of life has a built-in fizzle to it. The world's promise to deliver ultimate happiness, significance and satisfaction is at best inadequate and fleeting. One-time tennis great John McEnroe candidly remarked in an interview years ago, following his career, "I haven't quite figured out how to enjoy losing. As you get older, the pain of losing is greater, and the joy of winning is diminished."

One of the greatest tragedies of American history occurred on November 22, 1963—the assassination of John F. Kennedy. Reflecting on the assassination of Kennedy, Senator Daniel Patrick Moynihan made this astounding remark: "To be Irish is to know that in the end the world will break your heart." And in the end, we know that he is right. The world will break our hearts. In the end, death will trump even the most glorious earthly existence.

In his rhythmic ballad "Enough to Be on Your Way," singer and songwriter James Taylor provides an interesting backdrop chronicling the loss of his younger brother.

> My brother Alex died in '93 on (not for) my birthday. We all went down to Florida to say goodbye. The day after we flew home (the day after his cremation) a giant mother hurricane followed us north through the Carolina's [sic]; trashing everything in its path and finally raining record rains on Martha's Vineyard (home).
>
> In Paris, a year later I changed his character to a hippie chick named Alice and the location to Santa Fe; but my soulful older brother is still all over this song like a cheap suit.[5]

Taylor asks, along with all of us, is there a God in all of this futility? Does he care? Not only is Solomon's idea of God known only from nature and reason, but more significantly, he is a God of *silence*. He provides us very few answers in this book of wisdom, Ecclesiastes—only questions.

Having surveyed everything under the sun that promised to give lasting happiness and meaning, he waits until the end of the book to suggest the only thing that can transcend a world of futility and meaninglessness: our Creator. At last we are ready, if we ever intend to be, to look beyond earthly vanities to God, who made us for himself.

> Remember also your Creator in the days of your youth, before the evil days come and the years draw near when you will say, "I have no delight in them"; before the sun, the light, the moon, and the stars are darkened, and clouds

return after the rain. . . . Remember Him before the silver cord is broken and the golden bowl is crushed, the pitcher by the well is shattered and the wheel at the cistern is crushed; then the dust will return to the earth as it was, and the spirit will return to God who gave it. "Vanity of vanities," says the Preacher, "all is vanity!" (Ecclesiastes 12:1-2, 6-8)

This passage, one of the most poignant of all sequences of word pictures in the Old Testament, serves as a solemn reflection of a wise old man who has achieved wisdom through living. It is an eloquent allegory, the picture of a great house in decline that speaks of our mental as well as physical aging. Solomon then concludes his book with these powerful words: "The conclusion, when all has been heard, is: fear God and keep His commandments, because this applies to every person. For God will bring every act to judgment, everything which is hidden, whether it is good or evil" (Ecclesiastes 12:13-14).

Up to this point in the book, we have seen that all our paths and strivings come to nothing. And yet in this last chapter the Preacher sets us on a path that will not disappoint, the path toward some idea of a Creator God, who has numbered our few days on this earth. Here is the goal for which we were made, the Eternal toward whom the eternity of man's heart was intended to gravitate and find its home.

This is the driving force behind the words of the Preacher in Ecclesiastes. The world offers abundant pleasures and temporal happiness, but in the end, life adds up to futility and despair, because everything comes to *nothing*. Nada. It's almost as though Solomon is suggesting that we should taste of all that this world has to offer and, with it, the emptiness and futility, that we might seek a more lasting peace and happiness.

It should not be overlooked that most people in their thirties or younger often fail to grasp the fundamental message of Ecclesiastes. A person needs to mature a bit, be knocked down a bit, before he or she can see the seeming futility and disenchantment of all worldly efforts to be happy.

C. S. Lewis contended, however, that the grand pleasures of this life may be mere "drippings of grace," intended by God to whet our appetites, to awaken our thirst for eternal pleasures. Lewis referred to these pointers of pleasure in this temporal existence using the German word *Sehnsucht*, which we might translate as "inconsolable longings."

Perhaps these longings of the heart can be a reliable guide to what lies beyond this world, which is the theme that we will address in the next chapter.

The Heart Has Its Reasons

The Journey of Desire

Never lose a holy curiosity.

ALBERT EINSTEIN

Earth's crammed with heaven,
And every common bush aflame with God;
But only he who sees takes off his shoes,
The rest sit 'round and pluck blackberries.

ELIZABETH BARRETT BROWNING

There is a road from the eye to the heart
that does not go through the intellect.

G. K. CHESTERTON

Do you remember the Owl in *Alice's Adventures in Wonderland*? Alice sought out the Owl because she had heard that he had "the Answer." When she found him, she said, "It is said that you *alone* have the Answer."

The Owl replied, "My friend, as much as is said of me is true."

So she asked the Owl her question. And he answered carefully, "You must find out for yourself."

Alice said angrily, "Did I need the Owl to tell me I must think for myself?"

"But, my friend," the Owl replied. "That *is* the Answer."

The Owl hit on a fundamental principle that is so rare in our contemporary culture: the idea of thinking for *ourselves*. Perhaps in no other time has there been so great a need for clear thinking about the significant issues of life—Why are we here? Where are we going? Is there hope for life beyond the grave? Is there an afterlife? What *is* the Answer? Or can there even *be* answers to life's most important questions? What are we to make of this life?

Some time ago a friend sent me an e-mail that expresses a common sentiment: "LIFE IS A TEST. It is only a Test. If this were your actual life, you would have been given better instructions." We get a chuckle out of that, but the truth is that most of us wander through life searching for clues to make sense out of this life. Yet skepticism often prevails concerning answers to life's big questions. The modern world is deeply suspicious of anyone claiming to have *the* knowledge about transcendent affairs. Comedian and actor Steve Martin once captured the mood of our day when he declared, "It's so hard to believe anything anymore. . . . I guess I wouldn't believe in anything if it weren't for my lucky Astrology Mood Watch."

This was beautifully captured years ago in an interview with Woody Allen in the magazine *College People*. He mused, "More than any other time in history, mankind faces a crossroads. One path leads to despair and utter hopelessness. The other, to total extinction. Let us pray we have the wisdom to choose correctly."[1]

In one of the essays from his book *Without Feathers*, Allen questions the possibility of any kind of divine revelation as he spoofs his own Jewish roots, retelling the biblical story of Abraham and Isaac. As Allen tells the story, Abraham reports to his wife, Sarah, (and son Isaac) that God has commanded him to sacrifice their only son. Listen to this brooding dialogue as both Isaac and Sarah challenge Abraham to demonstrate how he knows for sure that he has heard from God:

> And Abraham awoke in the middle of the night and said to his only son, Isaac, "I have had a dream where the voice of the Lord sayeth that I must sacrifice my only son, so put your pants on."
>
> And Isaac trembled and said, "So what did you say? I mean when He brought this whole thing up?"
>
> "What am I going to say?" Abraham said. "I'm standing there at two a.m. in my underwear with the Creator of the Universe. Should I argue?"
>
> "Well, did he say why he wants me sacrificed?" Isaac asked his father.
>
> But Abraham said, "The faithful do not question. Now let's go because I have a heavy day tomorrow." And Sarah . . . said, "How doth thou know it was the Lord?" . . .
>
> And Abraham answered, "Because I know it was the Lord. It was a deep, resonant voice, well modulated, and nobody in the desert can get a rumble in it like that."[2]

Allen is known for his longtime disparagement of religion and his jesting about the faithful and believing community. And while it is cloaked in humor, Allen's imaginary dialogue between Abraham and Sarah is representative of our world's disdain for those who have a conviction about the idea of any kind of transcendent revelation.

A few years ago at Oxford University, I heard atheist Anthony Flew mock the very idea of the possibility of God having the ability to reveal himself through any kind of written revelation, such as the Bible. Like Flew, the longtime Oxford philosopher and atheist (whose works have been used as the classic texts for atheism for decades in universities in America and abroad), our world is deeply suspicious of any concept of God revealing his transcendent will to us. In many ways, our world, in its denial of any kind of transcendent perspective from a divine source, has succumbed to a "doglike" state of mind. The world looks only at the "pointers" in life, while refusing to consider the source.

A Doglike State of Mind

For many and varied reasons, our contemporary world has a suspicion of any kind of belief or faith in something that cannot be "proven" by science using the empirical method, which has become the controlling paradigm for all that is considered to be *true* knowledge. If something cannot be proven using the domain of scientific inquiry, it must be suspect and a part of religious dogma. In other words, the scientific community has often suggested that what we can verify through the physical senses is considered real and objective, while that which lies beyond the scope of the physical senses is considered spiritual, and therefore purely subjective, and a matter of faith or opinion.

While Flew doubts the very idea of divine revelation, in recent years he has had somewhat of a change of heart. His book *There Is a God*, co-written with philosopher Gary Habermas, chronicles his pilgrimage from atheism to theism over the past years. Flew essentially has come to believe that this world cannot be accounted for by the blind forces of fate and chance and that evidence suggests that there is a supreme being who is responsible for our world and existence.

When I heard Flew speak, he had been quick to point out that he would never become a Christian. Yet he was moved by the evidence suggesting a Grand Designer who has orchestrated our cosmos. To him, it is too simplistic and naïve to believe this world came into existence by mere chance. What he is suggesting in layman's terms is that the scientific community, which allows only for knowledge based on the "verification principle," is too simple, too reductionistic, in its methodology.

This reductionistic thinking was remarkably illustrated in the film *Expelled*, where economist and writer Ben Stein interviewed Richard Dawkins, a key proponent of a new vanguard of atheists and best known for his book *The God Delusion*. Try as he may to argue that only verifiable, empirical science can be the channel to true knowledge, Dawkins admitted to Stein at the end of the film, rather begrudgingly, that human life may have originated from alien dust from another planet or solar system. It's interesting that even an ardent atheist like Dawkins must look "beyond the stars" to account for the existence of life on our planet. And yet Dawkins chides Christians for their faith in a God who created the universe.

I remember as an undergraduate many years ago at the University of North Carolina at Chapel Hill, where I was a biology major, hearing about how blind evolutionary theory could somehow "explain" the origins and meaning of the universe. Even then, it seemed to me preposterous that some blind, random chance could account for the design and beauty of the cosmos.

C. S. Lewis addressed the blinding effect of such a reductionistic worldview in his essay "Transposition." He observed that a dog can't understand what you are doing when you point to his food. Invariably, he sniffs your finger rather than look down at the food. Lewis contended that our world, like the dog's world, is all fact and *no meaning*.

This world of all fact and no meaning that Lewis describes, a world of great knowledge but meager insight, was described nicely by Robert Short's observation that we have "lots of know-how, but little know-why; lots of sight, but little insight."

This dilemma of modernity was evidenced by one of the high priests of philosophy and science of the twentieth century, George Bernard Shaw. Toward the end of his life, he gave voice to the failure of his beloved science to find answers to life's ultimate questions:

> The science I pinned my faith to is bankrupt: . . . its counsels that were to have established the millennium have led straight to European suicide. And I—I who believed in it as no religious fanatic has ever believed in his superstition! For its sake I helped to destroy the faith of millions of worshippers in the temples of a thousand creeds. And now look at me and behold the supreme tragedy of the atheist who has lost his faith.[3]

Looking Through the Eye

For all of our culture's sophistication and knowledge and reliance on supposed science to answer life's questions, we are still left wanting for answers to *ultimate* questions. The great poet William Blake once wrote, "This Life's dim windows of the soul, distorts the Heavens from Pole to Pole, and leads you to believe a lie, when you see with, not through, the eye."[4]

This poem suggests that when we look only on the surface of things, reality may very well be distorted. Things are more than what they appear to be on the surface. And if not distorted, then at least minimized or trivialized. We need to look beneath the surface of the material world for answers to life's challenging questions.

Why? Because it is only beneath the surface of this visible world that ultimate, transcendent answers can be found. We, like Alice, need to ask the deep questions.

Listening to Our Hearts

In our modern world, which deals with surface answers to life's questions, where can we turn? If looking at the world only with our eyes (to use Blake's image) leads us to believe a lie, then perhaps we should look *through* the eye to see life as it really is. Or, to use Lewis's image, perhaps we should step *inside* to the transcendent nature of life. Both Blake and Lewis challenge us to look for clues to life's meaning through the "eye of faith."

Writers like Blake and Lewis are encouraging us to let our interior lives inform us about life. They are fundamentally challenging us to let our heart be our teacher and guide.

When we hear the word *heart*, we often make the mistaken assumption that the business of the heart is to feel emotions, but not to see or think. Blaise Pascal's most famous and probably most misunderstood dictum reads, "The heart has its reasons, of which reason knows nothing. . . . It is the heart which perceives God and not the reason. That is what faith is: God perceived by the heart, not by the reason."[5]

More often than not, Pascal's statement is understood as an argument favoring sentimentalism and subjectivism over reason. But Pascal was not suggesting that we jettison our thinking in favor of sentimentality. Rather, he was making the observation that learning and reason by themselves are cul-de-sacs and have their limits. There are an infinite number of things that go beyond human reason that help us make sense of life.

A classic dialogue from Harriet Beecher Stowe's *Uncle Tom's Cabin* perfectly captures this idea. In it, Tom, the slave, is talking to his skeptical owner, Augustine St. Clare, about his religious convictions following the death of St. Clare's devout daughter, Eva.

St. Clare: Who knows anything about anything? Was all
that beautiful love and faith only one of the ever-shifting
phases of human feeling, having nothing real to rest on,
passing away with the little breath? And is there no more
Eva,—no heaven,—no Christ,—nothing?

Tom: O, dear Mas'r, there is! I know it; I'm sure of it. Do,
do, dear Mas'r, believe it!

St. Clare: How do you know there's any Christ, Tom? You
never saw the Lord.

Tom: Felt Him in my soul, Mas'r,—feel Him now!

St. Clare: Tom, this is all real to you!

Tom: I can jest fairly see it, Mas'r.

St. Clare: I wish I had your eyes, Tom. But Tom, you know
that I have a great deal more knowledge than you; what if
I should tell you that I don't believe this Bible? Wouldn't it
shake your faith some, Tom?

Tom: Not a grain.[6]

You see, Tom was not advocating an anti-intellectual or even
a nonscientific approach to life. He was merely pointing out to
St. Clare that there is a knowledge that *transcends* the intellect
and mind, and it is the knowledge perceived from the heart.

The Vertical Search

If we allow our heart to guide us, it will intimate to us thoughts
of another world, possibly a world of peace and tranquility, a
world restored of the blight and havoc that we presently see.
Then the question must be asked, why are so few people listening to their hearts concerning these signals of transcendence,
to use sociologist Peter Berger's phrase? Perhaps the major

reason that many people do not listen to their hearts is because they are "sunk in the everydayness of life," as novelist Walker Percy describes Binx Bolling. Binx, the central character in his National Book Award-winning novel *The Moviegoer*, is a small-time stockbroker who lives quietly in suburban New Orleans, pursuing an interest in the movies, affairs with his secretaries and living out his days.

But Binx soon finds himself on a search for something more important, a discovery that will change his life forever. Listen to his words early in the novel:

> What is the nature of the search? . . . Really it is very simple. . . . The search is what anyone would undertake if he were not sunk in the everydayness of his life. . . . To become aware of the possibility of the search is to be onto something. Not to be onto something is to be in despair. . . . What do you seek—God? you ask with a smile. I hesitate to answer, since all other Americans have settled the matter for themselves. . . . Have 98% of Americans already found what I seek or are they so sunk in everydayness that not even the possibility of a search has occurred to them? On my honor, I do not know the answer.[7]

While Percy was musing decades ago, nothing has really changed, as most Americans today are in a similar fashion, "sunk in the everydayness of life." Essentially, we refuse to stop and reflect on the significant issues that we face, like God, life, death and the afterlife. Rather, we are trapped by the tyranny of the urgent. A little later in the same novel, Percy describes Uncle Jules with these insightful words:

> Uncle Jules is the only man I know whose victory in the world is total and unqualified. He has made a great deal of

money, he has a great many friends, he was Rex of Mardi Gras, he gives freely of himself and his money. He is an exemplary Catholic, but it is hard to know why he takes the trouble. For the world he lives in, the City of Man, is so pleasant that the City of God must hold little in store for him.[8]

Percy's words remind us to resist the inertia that so easily distracts us with the everydayness of our lives and to listen attentively to our *hearts*. They may indeed point to another world that awaits us.

A number of years ago, I was in England and had brought along with me the biography of C. S. Lewis written by the Oxford don A. N. Wilson. It was obvious that Wilson had a problem with Lewis's "muscular" Christianity. But then, in the 2009 issue of *New Statesman*, he recounted his "conversion," or return to theism, after a number of years of personal doubt and uncertainty. When I first heard this, I was deeply suspicious. But then I read his article "Why I Believe Again" and was genuinely moved by his "reconversion," if you will.

Here is how he first described the beginnings of his disbelief, as he was welcomed into the camp of the new atheists:

> As a hesitant, doubting, religious man I'd never known how they felt. But, as a born-again atheist, I now knew exactly what satisfactions were on offer. For the first time in my 38 years I was at one with my own generation. . . . Christopher Hitchens was excited to greet a new convert to his non-creed and put me through a catechism before uncorking some stupendous claret. "So—absolutely no God?" "Nope," I was able to say with Moonie-zeal.[9]

But as Wilson reflected deeply on his life and the people he had most greatly admired, he knew deep down that pure, unadulterated atheism was indeed too much to swallow:

> But religion, once the glow of conversion had worn off, was not a matter of argument alone. It involves the whole person. Therefore I was drawn, over and over again, to the disconcerting recognition that so very many of the people I had most admired and loved, either in life or in books, had been believers. . . . Watching a whole cluster of friends, and my own mother, die over quite a short space of time convinced me that purely materialist "explanations" for our mysterious human existence simply won't do—on an intellectual level.[10]

As he reflected on his life, Wilson experienced an epiphany as he began to ask questions with genuine honesty and candor. And can that question, or series of questions, be distilled down to the very idea of how we account for the human journey that we call *life*? Can unbridled materialistic atheism really account for our grand experience in this world? What do our hearts tell us about this search?

Wilson knew in his heart of hearts that pure, unadulterated materialism is a very thin soup indeed. This intuitive sixth sense—the *heart* Pascal spoke of—that Wilson believed so eloquently in, better explains the human drama.

I've got to confess that there are times when I wake up and wonder if all of life is some kind of accidental joke. Maybe something dreamed up by some celestial maverick to wreak havoc on his creatures. For if we always think life is easy or things will turn out the way we imagine, we will be sorely disappointed.

And still, deep down within my deepest soul's reflections, I have this inner compass that suggests to me that this isn't all a game. That somehow some infinite Designer is at work, preparing us for something more.

And instead of listening to the superficial thinking of modern naysayers, our hearts guide us toward another world that, deep down, we believe exists. And our desire for ultimate knowledge—to know the deep issues of life—is deeply embedded in the fabric of our human consciousness.

As we turn now to explore the various places of the heart where this knowledge of the transcendent is seen, maybe all along we are looking for some kind of afterlife. Maybe we are looking for what some people have called heaven.

Peter Kreeft has wisely observed:

> Many books have explored the heaven-shaped hole in the modern head, the meaninglessness of atheist and secularist philosophies. But there is not a single book in print whose main purpose is to explore the heart's longing for heaven. For the heart is harder to explore than the head and has had fewer explorers. The field of the heart has largely been left to the sentimentalists. But sentiments are only the heart's borders, not its inner country. We must discover this "undiscovered country."[11]

Cosmic Orphans

Our Sense of Alienation

It's not that I'm afraid to die.
I just don't want to be there when it happens.

WOODY ALLEN

If time were the wicked sheriff in a horse opera,
I'd pay for riding lessons and take his gun away.

W. H. AUDEN

When once you have got hold of a vulgar joke,
you may be certain that you have got
hold of a subtle and spiritual idea.

G. K. CHESTERTON

When we listen to our hearts, they suggest to us that we were made for something more, something that nothing in this world can satisfy. And one of the strongest pointers to something more is our sense of discord or alienation in the world. Try as we may, we are not really at home. Let's examine this idea briefly.

The British curmudgeon and one-time editor of *Punch* magazine, Malcolm Muggeridge, once declared that "to accept this world as a destination rather than a staging post would seem to me to reduce life to something too banal and trivial to be taken seriously or held in esteem." He came to this conclusion rather late in life, and one of the contributing factors (in addition to his encounter with Mother Teresa and her ministry in Calcutta among the poor) was his deep and abiding sense of alienation in this world. He writes,

> I had a sense, sometimes enormously vivid, that I was a stranger in a strange land; a visitor, not a native . . . a displaced person. . . . The feeling, I was surprised to find, gave me a great sense of satisfaction, almost of ecstasy. . . . The only ultimate disaster that can befall us, I have come to realize, is to feel ourselves to be at home here on earth. As long as we are aliens, we cannot forget our true homeland.[1]

Muggeridge's words serve as a tipping point, or signpost, to this idea of our alienation and estrangement with this world. While our sense of alienation manifests itself in numerous ways, let's consider briefly three examples: our fear of *death*, our uneasiness with *time*, and our sense of *humor*.

Our Fear of Death

Many years ago, the writer Joseph Bayly was flying from Chicago to Los Angeles and found himself engaged in conversation with an articulate middle-aged woman. "Where are you from?" he asked.

"Palm Springs," she answered.

Knowing Palm Springs to be a city of the rich and famous, he asked, "What's Palm Springs like?"

"Palm Springs is a beautiful place filled with unhappy people."

Curious about her unusual response, he posed the question "Are you unhappy?"

"Yes, I certainly am."

"Why?"

"I can answer it in one word: *mortality*. Until I was forty, I had perfect eyesight. Shortly after, I went to the doctor because I couldn't see as well as I could before. Ever since that time, these corrective glasses have been a sign to me that not only are my eyes wearing out, but I'm wearing out. Someday I'm going to die. I really haven't been happy since."

These words capture the feelings and angst of millions of Americans today. We don't want to be reminded that death will one day greet us, as it will everyone else in the human race. We don't want to lose this precious thing called life. And it's little consolation to imagine living on in the memory of our friends and loved ones. Woody Allen, in an interview with *Rolling Stone* magazine years ago, was being realistic when he declared, "Someone once asked me if my dream was to live on in the hearts of my people, and I said I would like to live on in my apartment. And that's really what I would prefer. . . . You drop dead one day, and it means less than nothing if billions of people are singing your praises every day, all day long."[2]

I'm reminded of the story of the English vicar who was asked by a colleague what he expected after death. He replied, "Well, if it comes to that, I suppose I shall enter into eternal bliss, but I really wish you wouldn't bring up such depressing subjects."

The Denial of Death
The words of the vicar express the prevalent response of our culture toward death. In a word, it is *denial*. Contemporary culture, having largely jettisoned the Judeo-Christian belief in an afterlife, nevertheless hates and fears death, and avoids the

subject like the plague. This denial of death takes on various guises in our culture.

One way is through aspirations to achieve immortality. A few years ago *Forbes* magazine reported that afterlife insurance is the newest thing in financial services. As more people request to be preserved by the ingenuity of cryonics, insurance companies such as New York Life are covering the costs. The concept of reviving a human embedded in ice was first developed as a story line for W. Clark Russell's 1887 yarn, "The Frozen Pirate." In 1974 the American Cryonics Society began freezing bodies, and now a half-dozen cryonics providers, such as the Scottsdale, Arizona-based Alcor Life Extension Foundation, promise to pickle their clients in liquid nitrogen in the hopes of bringing them back if and when technology allows. The tab? Fifty thousand dollars for the head, $120,000 for the whole body.

And if we cannot cheat death through achieving immortality, let's simply ignore the obvious. Society reasons, let's look at death in purely *naturalistic* terms. We are born, and then we die. Death is the most inconvenient thing in life, yet also the most obvious—like an elephant in the kitchen. Better to live like an ostrich with our head in the sand than to face the hard facts of mortality. In his critically acclaimed book *The Undertaking: Life Studies from the Dismal Trade*, Thomas Lynch laments the modern embarrassment over death with a curious analogy:

> The thing about the new toilet is that it removes the evidence in such a hurry. The flush toilet, more than any single invention, has "civilized" us in a way that religion and law could never accomplish. No more the morning office of the chamber pot or outhouse, where sights and sounds and odors reminded us of the corruptibility of flesh. . . . It is the same with our dead. We are embarrassed

by them in the way that we are embarrassed by a toilet that overflows the night that company comes. It is an emergency. We call the plumber.[3]

Muggeridge puts his finger on the real issue behind our denial of death when he writes:

It is, of course, inevitable that in a materialist society like ours death should seem terrible, and even inadmissible. If Man is the very apex of creation, with nothing greater than himself in the universe; if his earthly life exhausts the whole content of his existence, then, clearly, his definitive end, his death, is too outrageous to be contemplated, and so is better ignored.[4]

While today's culture denies the reality of death, the one sure thing about our mortal existence is that it will come to an end; the moment we are born, we begin to die. Samuel Beckett declared, "We give birth astride a grave." Alexander the Great is said to have directed that he be buried with his naked arm hanging out of his coffin, with his hand empty, to show one and all that the man who conquered the world left it as he entered it. Job in the Old Testament Scriptures declares, "Naked I came from my mother's womb, and naked I shall return there" (Job 1:21).

The Trivialization of Death

Because death has become such a taboo subject in modern culture, we seek diversions not only to make us happy, but also to keep us from reflecting on our mortality. When society cannot offer satisfying answers or explanations dealing with transcendent issues like our mortality, the tendency is to trivialize the matter.

There's a scene in the movie *Moonstruck* where Cher asks a

middle-aged man why middle-aged men chase after young women. He responds with the offhanded remark, "Maybe it's the fear of death." Cher stops dead in her tracks, reflects on the comment, and declares, "That's it!" Better to trivialize an issue that is too discomforting to talk about than to really come to grips with it.

In this manner, humor helps to allay our uneasiness with painful reminders of our mortality. *Prairie Home Companion* radio host Garrison Keillor once created a character who specifies that "his ashes be divided up and put in manila envelopes and mailed to people he admired, such as writers, actors, teachers, healers, religious people and rock stars—hundreds of them—as gifts."

Death is something so at odds with our human understanding, so tragic a thing to contemplate, that more often than not, we trivialize it or make jokes about it. It's the way we cope with it as human beings.

Hope Beyond the Grave

While modern culture attempts to deny death by wishing it away or ignoring it, from earliest times humanity has tenaciously believed in an afterlife. We might go so far as to say that part of our humanness is to desire an afterlife, even as we face death.

I recall visiting the British Museum in London, where an entire floor is dedicated to the Egyptians' practice of mummification to preserve their royalty for the journey to the world beyond. However various the forms, belief in an afterlife is coterminous with humanity.

While many tell us to accept death as "natural," the truth of the matter is that deep down we resist such a notion. Why? Because we feel a sense of dissonance with death. In fact, we are immortals trapped in mortal surroundings, our bodies. While the pop psychologists of our day try to convince us that death is just another stage of growth, deep down we resist such a calm assessment. Such advice from our therapeutic professionals is "like telling a quadriplegic that paralysis is a stage of exercise, or a divorcée that divorce is a stage of marriage. It's the kind of joke only a moron or a sadist would tell."[5]

While modernity seeks to deny death, in earlier Victorian times—with a decidedly Christian worldview—death was perceived differently. Death was magnified, talked about and even relished. British author Paul Johnson observes,

> The Victorians with their death-masks, their elaborate funeral processions and carriages . . . looked death squarely and ceremoniously in the face. Deathbed scenes were elaborately recorded or committed to memory, and became part of family folklore, reverently told to children and grandchildren. . . . Death was a domestic, household, family affair, with the dying person upstairs in a well-attended bedroom with a fire in the grate, people downstairs walking softly and talking in whispers, straw in the street outside to muffle the noise of carriage-wheels, the neighbors alerted to the impending event and sending regular and anxious enquiries.[6]

Even in such secular times as our own, those of us in the West with our traditional belief in the afterlife seem obsessed with ritually denying what obviously happens. We embalm our corpses, dress them up in new suits, pronounce last rites over them and bury them in airtight caskets and concrete vaults to postpone the inevitable decay. Through our rituals we act out our stubborn reluctance to yield to this most powerful of human experiences.

John Updike often muses in his writings about our mortality and what may lie beyond this temporal existence. In his Pulitzer Prize-winning *Rabbit at Rest*, he penned one of the funniest novels ever written about death. In his fourth and final appearance, Harry "Rabbit" Angstrom, Updike's jockish alter ego, munches various junk foods that thicken his body while thinning his arteries as he makes his way toward his Maker.

Updike himself seems to be having a wonderful time contemplating eternity with his wistful observations about the afterlife that come out of Rabbit's mouth. At one point, while Rabbit looks for his car at a Florida airport, the narrator deep within Rabbit's consciousness thinks to himself, "He doesn't remember which of these rows he parked the car in. He parked it in the patch of dead blank brain cells like all of our brains will be when we're dead unless the universe has cooked up some truly elaborate surprise."[7]

Our Uneasiness with Time

One of the Grimms's fairy tales, "The Duration of Life," tells the story of God originally determining thirty years as the ideal life span for all animals, including humankind. The donkey, dog and monkey all consider it much too long, however, and beg God to reduce their years by eighteen, twelve and ten. The man, being healthy, vigorous and somewhat greedy, asks to be given those extra years. God agrees, so man's years total seventy.

The first thirty are his own and pass quickly. The next eighteen are the donkey years, during which he has to carry countless burdens on his back. Then come the dog years, twelve years when he can do little but growl and drag himself along. And finally, the monkey years, his closing ten, when he grows strange and does things that make children laugh at him.

While the tale suggests that the latter years of a person's life are painful, we still yearn to see no end to our days. We have an uneasiness with time and are startled at the concept of time—or rather at its passing.

In his book *When I Relax I Feel Guilty*, Tim Hansel recalls reading the thought-provoking article entitled "If You Are 35, You Have 500 Days to Live." Its thesis was that when you subtract the time spent sleeping, working, tending to personal matters, hygiene, odd chores, medical care, eating, traveling and miscellaneous time-stealers, in the next thirty-six years you will have roughly the equivalent of only five hundred days left to spend as you wish.

One of the most creative treatments of time is found in a wonderfully odd and beguiling inquiry, that of physicist Alan Lightman, who teaches physics and writing at Massachusetts Institute of Technology. He has written the highly acclaimed work *Einstein's Dreams*. Set in Bern, Switzerland, in 1905, the book tells of a young patent clerk named Albert Einstein who has been dreaming marvelous dreams about the nature of time and has almost finished his special theory of relativity. What were his dreams during those last pivotal few months? In this enchanting work, thirty fables conjure up as many theoretical realms of time dreamt in as many nights.

In one of these vignettes, Lightman portrays how the people of Bern attempt to slow the passing of time by curious means. In this particular world, it's apparent that something is a bit odd. No houses are visible in the valleys or plains. Everyone lives in the mountains. At some time in the past, Lightman suggests, scientists discovered that time actually flows more slowly the farther one is from the center of the earth. And while the effect is minuscule, it can be measured with extremely sensitive instruments.

Once the phenomenon was determined, some people, anxious to stay young, moved to the mountains. Now all houses are built on Dom, the Matterhorn, Monte Rosa and other high ground, so that it is virtually impossible to sell living quarters anywhere else. And because many people are no longer content simply to locate their homes on a mountain, to get the maximum effect they have constructed their houses on stilts.

In another fable, dated 28 June 1905, a family is having a picnic on the bank of the Aare, ten kilometers south of Bern. A young man, his wife and his grandmother sit on a blanket, eating smoked ham, cheese, sourdough bread with mustard, grapes and chocolate cake. As they eat and drink, and the couple's daughters frolic in the grass, a gentle breeze comes over the river, and they breathe in the summer air.

Then something arrests their attention. Suddenly, a flock of birds flies overhead. The young man leaps from the blanket to chase after them. He is soon joined by others, who have spotted the birds from the city. One bird alights in a tree, and a woman climbs the trunk, attempting to catch it, but it jumps to a higher branch. As the woman hangs helplessly in the tree, another bird is seen eating seeds on the ground. Two men sneak up behind it, carrying a giant bell jar. But the bird takes to the air, joining the rest of the flock. Now the birds fly through the town.

Lightman describes the significance of the birds:

> This flock of nightingales is time. Time flutters and fidgets and hops with these birds. Trap one of these nightingales beneath a bell jar and time stops. . . . The children, who alone have the speed to catch the birds, have no desire to stop time. For the children, time moves too slowly already. . . . The elderly desperately wish to halt time, but are much too slow and fatigued to entrap any bird.[8]

Lightman's playful novel beautifully portrays how we try to slow down time, to savor this life. And we are reminded of the sobering truth that as time marches on, our joys and cherished dreams are ruined or come to nothing. This isn't really cynicism so much as it is realism. We can't slow down time. And as time passes, we are amazed how quickly it goes.

In a letter to Sheldon Vanauken, a struggling student of his at Oxford University, C. S. Lewis penned the following thoughtful words:

> You say the materialist universe is "ugly." I wonder how you discovered that! If you are really a product of a materialistic universe, how is it you don't feel at home there? Do fish complain of the sea for being wet? Or if they did, would that fact itself not strongly suggest that they had not always been, or [would] not always be, purely aquatic creatures? Notice how we are perpetually surprised at Time. ("How time flies! Fancy John being grown-up and married! I can hardly believe it!") In heaven's name, why? Unless, indeed, there is something in us which is not temporal.[9]

We see then, that both our fear of *death* and our uneasiness with *time* witness to our being strangers in this world. We encounter frequent hints of the world to come, but they are transitory and ephemeral. Nobody ever gets into the secret garden. The closest we ever get to it is in some hint of an echo that we hear in a concerto or see in a beautiful face or painting, which fills us with a deep sadness. It is lost for now, and we must turn back to our traffic jams and enemas and red tape.[10]

Our Sense of Humor

A third clue, or pointer, to our alienation and discord in this world is humor. Some have even suggested that a natural theology of "another world" can be argued from the human phenomenon of coarse jokes. Invariably, these jokes tend to dwell almost entirely on the processes of excretion and reproduction, two of the most "natural" acts that we perform. While we share these processes with all other creatures, we joke and guffaw about such activities because they seem utterly unnatural, even comical.

And although we attempt to veil or guard such functions, it has been observed that no one has ever witnessed embarrassment or shame among the animals as they perform these commonplace functions. Can you imagine a horse, dog or cat shy about the need to excrete in public or reluctant to perform reproductive functions in broad daylight?

Despite all the attempts by atheists to make the human race nothing more than a glorified animal at the apex of the evolutionary continuum, deep down our souls seem to resonate with discord, which hints that we may in fact be made for more than this world.

It may be that the only good reason to find humor in such seemingly crude phenomena as sex, death, burping and breaking wind is that they parody our mortal existence. As G. K. Chesterton observed in his essay "Wine When It Is Red," "If it is not true that a divine being fell, then one can only say that one of the animals went completely off its head!" That is, the Christian has a great advantage over other people, not by being less fallen than they or less doomed to live in a fallen world, but by *knowing* that he or she is a fallen person in a fallen world. In a way, then, laughter has much in common with prayer, for in both acts we are acknowledging ourselves as fallen creatures.

Along these same lines, it's interesting to observe that classic materialists who look to this world alone to bring fulfillment and happiness are frequently those who rarely display joy and laughter. Life is too serious to be joked about, they reason. In fact, people who take themselves too seriously (those of the ilk of Charles Darwin, Bertrand Russell, Karl Marx, Bill Gates, Richard Dawkins or Christopher Hitchens) fail to grasp the irony that informs our human affairs. This biting irony is written into our mortal existence and is beautifully described by Muggeridge in his book *The End of Christendom*:

> This irony . . . [is] conveyed beautifully in the medieval cathedrals, where you have the steeple climbing up into the sky symbolizing all the wonderful spiritual aspirations of human beings, but at the same time, set in the same roof, you have these little grinning gargoyles staring down at the earth. The juxtaposition of these two things might seem strange at first. But I contend that they are aspects of the same essential attitude of mind, an awareness that at the heart of our human existence there is this mystery. Interwoven with our affairs is this wonderful spirit of irony which prevents us from ever being utterly and irretrievably serious.[11]

In many ways, then, humor has much to say about humility because it manifests itself in the incongruities of life. Few things are as absurd as people attempting to be God. And while the medieval world had court jesters and grinning gargoyles on cathedral roofs and carved into the ends of the pews to remind worshipers of human pride, the modern world has largely lost these transcendent reminders. As Muggeridge once observed, it is significant that our urban high-rise buildings have no gargoyles—truly, modernity takes itself quite seriously.

Maybe this is why Garrison Keillor once observed, "Some people think it's difficult to believe in God and to laugh, but I think it's the other way around. God writes a lot of comedy—it's just that he has so many bad actors."

Celebrating the Daily Humdrum

Either all of life is sacred,
or none of it is sacred.

MALCOLM MUGGERIDGE

Do not forget that the value
and interest of life is not so much to do
conspicuous things . . . as to do ordinary things
with the perception of their enormous value.

PIERRE TEILHARD DE CHARDIN

Still another telling "signal of transcendence" that we are made for another world lies right beneath our nose and is what we might simply refer to as the "humdrum," the living out of our mundane, ordinary lives. This sign may be the most profound, but by the same token, the least obvious.

Such a view of life sees everything that we do—literally, everything "under the sun"—as having a sacramental perspective. What do we mean by sacramental? *Webster's New Collegiate Dictionary* suggests that *sacrament* derives from the Latin verb *sacrare*, meaning "to consecrate," and the noun form suggests something that is a sign or symbol of a spiritual reality.

So to say that all of life has a sacramental perspective is to envision all our affairs—our eating and drinking, our working and playing, our loving and serving—as being reminders of transcendent mysteries. Granted, these ordinary routines have their appointed functions, but a sacramental perspective infuses the daily humdrum with a more profound meaning.

A sacramental perspective that imbues all of life is at odds with the prevailing secular notion of life, which tends to leech any kind of transcendent notion from our existence. This mindset, as we saw earlier, is largely the result of the approach of scientism, which embraces the belief that there are no divine mysteries in life and that everything can be exhaustively explained according their natural function.

Such a sacramental outlook on life is in many respects closer to the ancients than to most twenty-first-century people. The ancient believed that he walked in the presence of the Unseen, that this world is a sign of divine mysteries. Even those among us with a religious penchant struggle with truly seeing ourselves as walking daily among the hallowed—that is, seeing ourselves as living in the presence of divine mysteries as we carry out the commonplace routines of daily living. We all too often make a distinction between the secular and the sacred.

We constantly put the supposed Big Things in life (like religious worship, sacrifice and mystery) into the *religious* arena and then relegate the bulk of our lives (like eating, meeting others socially, etc.) into the *secular* arena. But when we embrace a truly sacramental perspective of life, *everything* matters. As Malcolm Muggeridge observed, "Either all of life is sacred, or none of it is sacred."

The Mystery of Manners

One aspect of the daily humdrum charged with transcendent

overtones is the practice of courtesy and manners. Why do we have manners? What is the basis of our showing courtesy to one another? What is the origin of the belief that we are to treat others with dignity and respect?

C. S. Lewis began his classic work *Mere Christianity* with the observation that there is a moral *oughtness* that informs our human existence. We know the right thing to do, Lewis argues, and we know that we are supposed to treat others with dignity and respect. But there is a second universal—namely, that none of us are really keeping this "Law of Nature":

> This year, or this month, or, more likely, this very day, we have failed to practice ourselves the kind of behavior we expect from other people. There may be all sorts of excuses for us. . . . The question at the moment is not whether they are good excuses. The point is that they are one more proof of how deeply, whether we like it or not, we believe in the Law of Nature.[1]

As Lewis suggests, it almost goes without saying that we often find ourselves coming up short—transgressors of this moral *oughtness*—when it comes to treating people with the respect they deserve. One of the most memorable put downs of all time involved the inimitable Winston Churchill and took place at a dinner party toward the conclusion of a heated exchange between Churchill and Lady Astor. She chided him, "Mr. Churchill, you are drunk," to which he replied, "And you, madam, are ugly. But I shall be sober tomorrow."

Let's examine this idea of manners and courtesy in more detail. What is the origin of manners? Take the word *courtesy*, which comes from the word *court*. The court carries with it the idea of the residence or establishment of a sovereign, and to be "courteous" means, if we look in any dictionary, to be marked by polished manners, or to be gallant, or to be especially respectful. Therefore, to treat others courteously is to show them the dignity and respect appropriate for the court. In other words, when we treat others with dignity and respect, we are treating them like royalty.

We appear to inhabit a world where, at the very heart of our courtesy and respect for others, there exists the deep-seated belief that people deserve this respect, not necessarily because they have earned it, but because they are fellow human beings. Interestingly, all the major religions of the world attach a certain sacredness and dignity to human life. We extend courtesy and respect to one another because people are important. People matter.

Civility: Taking a Turn for the Worse

In recent years, however, civility and manners have taken a turn for the worse and have become a hot topic in our national conversation. With the hectic pace of American life, some would argue that it's becoming more difficult to show courtesy to others. It has been suggested that in a lifetime, the average American will spend six months sitting at stop lights, eight months opening junk mail, one year looking for misplaced objects, two years unsuccessfully returning phone calls and five years waiting in lines. It's little wonder that no one believes he or she has time to be courteous.

In his thought-provoking book *A Short History of Rudeness: Manners, Morals, and Misbehavior in Modern America*, social critic Mark Caldwell gives a history of the demise of manners and the triumphant "progress" of rudeness in America. Predictably, as the breakdown of civility has become a national obsession, it has led to the rise of etiquette watchdogs like Miss Manners and Martha Stewart to deliver us from this onslaught of nastiness.

In his witty and engaging book *Say Please, Say Thank You*, Donald McCullough gives us gentle reminders of how to make this world a better place by taking advantage of simple opportunities to treat others with dignity and respect. The simple things—like saying "please" and "thank you," picking up the check for dinner, not being late for appointments, dressing appropriately for occasions and writing notes of appreciation—demonstrate respect and honor to the people in our lives.

Civility and Clothes: Is There a Connection?

One of the most interesting and subtle ways that manners have run amok is revealed in our clothing. In recent years, we have witnessed a more casual approach to dressing for the workplace, to say the least. This has evolved to the point that we now even use the term *dress-down Friday*.

While many embrace this new casualness in the workplace, casual dress may subtly convey to others and ourselves that what we are doing can also be taken casually. There appears to be an erosion of symbols that once lent a certain dignity to the person. In years gone by, specific types of clothing meant something. But now casual clothes are deemed appropriate for all occasions.

In a bygone era, it seems clothes were symbolic of a certain dignity and propriety that fit the occasion, whether it was work, athletics, weddings or funerals. In that world, the Old Myth prevailed. Things *mattered*, so we dressed appropriately for the occasion. But with the advent of the New Myth, these symbols are being dismissed as being old-fashioned and out-of-date. To modernity, they smack too much of hierarchy for our educated sensibilities. The modern world prefers to be "flattened out," removing all distinctions between people.

But clothes *do* matter. The way we dress for different occasions reveals not only our attitude about whatever we are doing (work, worship, play), but also our respect (or lack thereof) for others.

The story is told of Cecil Rhodes, the South African statesman and financier (for whom the Rhodes Scholarship is named), who was known for being a stickler for proper dress. As he was hosting a formal dinner one evening and about to welcome his guests (who were all wearing full evening dress), he was told about one of his guests, a young man who had arrived by train without the opportunity to change from his travel-stained clothes.

Rhodes disappeared, leaving the guests to wonder what had happened to him. He eventually returned to the dinner party wearing a shabby old suit so his young guest would not feel uncomfortable. Rhodes's gesture demonstrates that the clothes we wear can actually be a means of showing grace, favor and hospitality to the people around us.

Clothes often reflect the demeanor of the wearer. They *signify* something. A story from the world of the famed Neiman Marcus store illustrates this point well. As the story goes, a well-meaning customer was prompted to send Stanley Marcus the following letter:

Dear Mr. Marcus:

I have been receiving beautiful and expensive brochures from you at regular intervals. It occurs to me that you might divert a little of the fortune you must be spending for this advertising matter to raise the salaries of your more faithful employees. For instance, there's an unassuming, plainly dressed little man on the second floor who always treats me with extreme courtesy when I visit your store and generally persuades me to buy something I don't really want. Why don't you pay him a little more? He looks as though he could use it.

Yours truly, Mrs. WS

By return mail came Marcus's reply:

> Dear Madam:
>
> Your letter impressed us so deeply that we called a directors' meeting immediately, and thanks solely to your own solicitude, voted my father a $20-a-week raise.
>
> Yours truly,
> Stanley Marcus

While such displays of humility often go unnoticed, we are still reminded that our dress says a lot about the kind of people we are and what we think of others. And while civility, manners and common courtesy may continue to deteriorate, their abiding presence in our lives signifies that people are important. And because they are important, we do well to treat others with the dignity and honor they are entitled to, not because they have earned it, but because they are fellow human beings.

The Hallowed Home

In addition to the daily rituals of civility and manners, another aspect that bears the hint of transcendence is found in the home. It is in the home, where ordinary daily living transpires, that the celebration of these mysteries occurs and is to be offered up in sacrificial service to God. It is in the family household—with all its eating and drinking, working and playing, serving and loving—that these hints of the transcendent are observable.

The home, which represents the family—with the corresponding themes of men and women, children, sex and marriage—is a central element in the vision of G. K. Chesterton. Amid the moral problems that our society faces, his writings in defense of the home as a transcendent institution continue to provide a needful remedy to a confused world.

Alvaro de Silva offers the following observation on Chesterton's defense of the family in his introduction to a collection of Chesterton's writings on the family:

> Gilbert K. Chesterton (1874-1936) thought that the Victorians had lost "the sense of the sacredness of the home." The succeeding generation tried to get rid of the home altogether. Now we hunger and search for it everywhere. For some, a cat will do, or a dog or an expensive fur or a cheap affair with a stranger. . . . We are spiritual barbarians and emotional nomads. In our despair, we put two broken umbrellas together and call it home sweet home. . . . Thus our expectations of a home have become one of the most important decoys in advertising. Every conceivable commercial product is supposed to remind buyers about the delights and offerings of "family." Respect, caring, understanding, sharing, loyalty, freedom, love, joy and a smile or two are now being offered as readily available outside, at the bank or at the hardware store, because these commodities are found less and less at home. Despite the efforts to find one, there is no alternative to the family.[2]

Few have written as passionately or as provocatively on the importance and sacredness of the family as Chesterton. To him, the family mirrors what is truly important in life. The family images the things that really matter, because "the business done in the home is nothing less than the shaping of the bodies and souls of humanity. The family is the factory that manufactures mankind."[3]

Even the writer Aldous Huxley once envisioned such a dark world and suggested that there would be a time when marriage would be treated in a cavalier manner. He addressed this in the preface to *Brave New World*, when he declared, "Marriage licenses will be sold like dog licenses, good for a period of twelve months, with no law against changing dogs or keeping more than one animal at a time."

But Chesterton himself was a realist. He saw the marriage relationship between husband and wife as the foundation of the family, and this family is a picture of the spiritual drama being played out in our world:

> When we defend the family we do not mean it is always a peaceful family; when we maintain the thesis of marriage we do not mean that it is always a happy marriage. We mean that it is the theatre of the spiritual drama, the place where things happen, especially the things that matter. It is not so much the place where a man kills his wife as the place where he can take the equally sensational step of not killing his wife.[4]

Different Rooms in the Sacred House

While we are indebted to Chesterton for his contributions to our understanding of the sacramental aspect of the family, we might go even further to reflect on how the *house* represents the transcendent dimensions of life. As we carry out normal and routine affairs of daily living, the ordinary gives way to the mystery. When we discharge our daily, menial tasks, they are fraught with spiritual overtones.

The architecture of a house, with its various rooms associated with their functions, gives us a picture of the diversity that we observe in all of life. And when we observe distinctions between rooms according to their various functions, we are granting them the appropriate dignity and honor befitting them.

Author Thomas Howard provides an excellent study of the sacramental aspect of the different rooms of a house in his book *Hal-*

lowed Be This House.[5] Let's examine a few of the rooms more closely.

The entryway. Consider the entryway, or front door, of a house. It's simply a place for passing through, as we are always en route when we are in the entryway. Yet today our coming and going is rarely through the front door of a house, but rather through the garage with its maze of garden equipment, lawn mowers, washing machines and winter jackets. We even greet many of our guests by this route, with the casual remark, "Well, they're just family, anyway." In another era, the entryway served as a reminder that before you could "let down," you had to get farther into the house. So then, the entryway of a house suggests that the home *ought* to be a place of order and grace.

The living room. What about the living room? While no particular activity is specifically attached to it, when we think of the living room we generally think of families gathering to be together for conversation or entertaining. The living room portrays what families are all about—the glorious enterprise of husband and wife committing themselves to the daunting task of raising children to be upstanding and dedicated members of society. Certainly, raising children is no simple task.

I love the way Garrison Keillor portrays the challenge of raising a daughter:

> The father of a daughter, for example, is nothing but a high-class hostage. A father turns a stony face to his sons, berates them, shakes his antlers, paws the ground, snorts, runs them off into the underbrush, but when his daughter puts her arm over his shoulder and says, "Daddy, I need to ask you something," he is a pat of butter in a hot frying pan. The butter thinks to itself, "This time I really am going to remain rectangular," and then it feels very relaxed, and then it smells smoke.[6]

Those of us who have sons and daughters can definitely appreciate Keillor's insights, which address the challenges we face in the living room. The living room images what family members, bound by flesh and blood, have the opportunity to begin learning together. And the lesson is applicable to the entire human race—the lesson of love, or charity. In the family, husbands and wives, sons and daughters, begin to learn about genuine love—that self-giving, freedom and joy are part of a sacred dance that portrays what our lives are to be.

The dining room. The dining room speaks of greater things than the mere consumption of food. And while eating may occur in any room of the house, clearly much more is going on in our meals than the mere function of getting physical nourishment for our bodies. From a utilitarian perspective, our nourishment might be achieved with pills or liquids or needles (as is done when people are sick and unable to eat for themselves), but such arrangements normally will simply not do.

No, we humans prefer to *ceremonialize* our eating. Take the simple meal, not just the fancy rehearsal dinner for a wedding that you may have in mind. We mark this three-times-repeated daily ritual with certain formalities, no matter how seemingly insignificant. We prefer our food to be neatly arranged on our plate and not simply jumbled together (unless it is a soup or stew), and we consider it proper that everyone wait until the others are served before we begin. And we enjoy a bit of color in the presentation of the meal, perhaps some red tomatoes along with the green vegetables, and we find a bouquet of flowers on the table aesthetically pleasing.

Certainly the advent of fast food and the hectic pace in our culture have seriously undermined our attempts to make eating more than the mere transfer of food to the body. We see people eating standing up in the food courts at malls, eating in their cars as they drive down the expressway and eating at their desks in the workplace.

Yet we often still find ourselves attempting to eat our meals with some amount of dignity and decorum. Chances are, even when we are by ourselves, we do not stand over the stove and shovel the food out of the skillet directly into our mouths. Eating expresses something profound, and when we adorn it with ritual, we give it dignity. It's a signal that things matter, that they are worth something, that they are significant. We are intimating that this commonplace activity is more than the thing itself.

Perhaps behind the activity of eating is the picture of community and fellowship with one another. When we set apart the business of eating from the rest of the household functions and approach it (particularly the evening meal) as the occasion when men, women and children gather together, is this not a gathering together to enact our common humanness? When we think about the most joyful occasions of our lives, were they not frequently focused around dining with close friends and relatives? Is there not an almost sacred aspect to these gatherings? Is there any surprise that most of the major religions of the world include eating as a central element in their faith? Do these gatherings not in fact resemble holy feasts?

The kitchen. As lifestyles have grown more casual, and gadgets and appliances have grown more high-tech, the kitchen has not been one of the rooms we parade before our friends. It tends to be behind the scenes, where preparation and cleanup are performed, but rarely is it center stage. We prepare a meal for the occasion, and when the meal begins, the work of preparation is put out of sight. The same is true of cleaning the kitchen and the utensils employed. The cleanup looks in retrospect to the meal just finished and is not the thing itself.

The kitchen may best reflect the dignity and role of service, because service's whole reason for existence is to prepare for something, and it is never an end in itself. Service finds itself waiting in relative obscurity for the next job. And when we carry out our daily routines of service around the household, we're playing out the drama of charity. While most of us strive after power, glory and prestige as being the most important things of life, service perhaps lies closest to the heart of what really matters in the sacred drama. Service may in fact tell us a lot about life beyond this temporal world.

The bathroom. And what in the world are we to make of the bathroom? Certainly if we say almost anything about the bathroom, it will make us anxious. And it isn't just the Victorians who sought to go behind closed doors for such private activities. Throughout human civilization, there has been a perpetual need for privacy. It may be worth asking where this tradition—this human preoccupation with concealment—came from?

As unpopular and antiquated a notion as it may seem, could this need for "covering" be our innate sense of shame? Could it be that this desire for privacy is nothing other than a desire to keep veiled what ought to be veiled? Do our attitude and behavior not serve as a litmus test of how seriously we take this sense of shame?

Our society revels in a *laissez-faire* attitude that seeks to make nothing private, nothing veiled. Everything, we are told, is to be open before the watching world. Such an open discourse has historically been considered taboo. This worldview of frankness suggests that the only way to transcend the Victorian priggishness and to liberate society to its truly "natural and free" expression is to fight anything that smacks of censorship or fidelity.

Yet in his brilliant analysis of the history of Western culture, *Forbidden Knowledge*, Roger Shattuck raises serious concerns about our quest for knowledge amid the explosion of scientific knowledge and the increasing problem of pornography:

> Are there things we should not know? Can anyone or any institution, in this culture of unfettered enterprise and growth, seriously propose limits on knowledge? Have we lost the capacity to perceive and honor the moral dimensions of such questions? . . . What has happened to the venerable notion of forbidden knowledge? In the practicalities of daily living, we accept constraints ranging from environmental regulations to truancy laws to traffic lights. In matters of the mind and its representations, Western thinkers and institutions increasingly reject limits of any kind as unfounded and stultifying. . . . Both scientific research and the worlds of art and entertainment rely on an unspoken assumption that total freedom in exchanging symbolic products of mind need not adversely affect the domain of daily living and may well enhance it.[7]

While such an "enlightened" worldview sees no proper limits to knowledge and no need for privacy, an idea of old says otherwise. Not everyone is warranted to be seeing everything or going everywhere. Behind every closed door, behind every taboo, behind every veil, behind every prohibitive "Thou shall not," there is something at work that tells me that I am not allowed in.

There are limits. We are sometimes excluded, discriminated against, because we don't have the right to "go in."

No, such superficial frankness will not do. Possibly our need for privacy displays our mortality and vulnerability. When we close the bathroom door, we show our membership card in the club universal, perhaps reminiscent of a lost Paradise.

In this chapter, we have seen how there is a palpable sacramental aspect in the ordinary. The daily humdrum—our courtesy and manners, the family, daily living in the home—means something more, something greater, than mere *function*. We celebrate the ordinary because all of life is sacred, even the most ordinary and mundane of our affairs.

They all carry the scent of another world.

- 6 -

Transcendence in Our Work

❦

And the wind shall say:
here were a decent, godless people,
Their only monument, an asphalt road
and a thousand lost golf balls.

T. S. ELIOT

Men lust, but they know not what for;
they wander, and lose track of the goal; they chase
power and glory, but miss the meaning of life.

GEORGE GILDER

Work is not, primarily, a thing one does to live,
but the thing one lives to do.

DOROTHY SAYERS

Work. We love it and hate it, but we can't do without it. These writers' sentiments express the genuine ambivalence that we often have about work.

- Mark Twain declared, "I do not like work even when someone else does it."

- Robert Frost opined, "By working faithfully eight hours a day, you may eventually get to be a boss and work twelve hours a day."
- Charles Baudelaire mused, "Everything considered work is less boring than amusing oneself."
- Paul Valery observed, "A businessman is a hybrid between a dancer and a calculator."

Despite the vast number of waking hours that we devote to work, work's purpose—and what it signifies—is rarely considered. Observing the alienation that pervades many contemporary, affluent, industrialized societies, the noted psychologist Victor Frankl pondered the plight of those who "have enough to live by, but not enough to live for, who seemed to have the means, but no meaning."

As Frankl suggests, our age is one when we often have the means, but little or no *meaning*. Essentially, this is because we have abdicated the transcendent dimension of work. The truth is that we work for more than money and for far more profound reasons than we might imagine. Work itself is another pointer toward something more than simply work itself.

But let's first look at the confusion over the meaning and purpose of work that informs the contemporary landscape. Arguably, in no other time in recent history have there been more cataclysmic changes than in the workplace landscape—not only in recent decades, but especially in the economic recession of a few years ago. And coupled with the catastrophic events in our nation known as 9/11, many have wondered about the meaning and purpose of work.

Crisis in the Workplace
Certainly in our day we have witnessed monumental changes in

the workplace. With the general movement from an industrial to an informational and technological economy in the West, and the consequent rise of entrepreneurial businesses, the measure of success as well as why we work is perhaps being discussed more than in any other time in American history.

The workplace is no longer the relatively safe, secure haven it once was. Just as Freud made the famous cry of resignation, "Women, what do they want?" men, who have traditionally defined themselves by the ability to bring home the paycheck, are now often asking the question, What do men *really* want?

And because the workplace has seen a great influx of women in recent decades, coupled with the economic downturn and downsizing and reorganization, instability has become the accepted norm of corporate America. Men in particular no longer look at work—or life—in the same light. Many would suggest that the contemporary man lacks a firm self-identity, and even manhood now finds itself under assault.

In *The Book of Guys*, Garrison Keillor laments man's current state of affairs, especially as it relates to how he is perceived by women.

> Years ago, manhood was an opportunity for achievement, and now it is a problem to overcome. Plato, St. Francis, Michelangelo, Mozart, Leonardo da Vinci, Vince Lombardi, Van Gogh—you don't find guys of that caliber today. . . . They are trying to be Mr. O.K. All-Rite, the man who can bake a cherry pie, go play basketball, come home, make melon balls and whip up a great soufflé, converse easily about intimate matters, participate in recreational weeping, laugh, hug, be vulnerable, be passionate in a skillful way, and the next day go off and lift them bales into that barge and tote it. A guy who women consider Ac-

ceptable. Being all-rite is a dismal way to spend your life, and guys are not equipped for it anyway. . . . A man is like a bear riding a bicycle: he can be trained to do it but he would rather be in the woods, doing what bears do.[1]

Even the meaning of success is being evaluated in a different light. Sociologist Michael Kimmel, writing in the *Harvard Business Review*, addresses this new paradigm of work when he notes that the contemporary man's view of success is quite different from his predecessors. More specifically, "Few men today fit the traditional picture of the distant father, patriarchal husband, and work-obsessed breadwinner. Yet neither have many dropped out of the working world to participate in full-time daddydom."[2]

While Kimmel's work that appeared in *Harvard Business Review* and later in his book *Manhood in America: A Cultural History*, was penned over fifteen years ago, nothing much has changed in terms of the fundamental questions of identity and purpose that surface in the workplace at every level. Kimmel contends that today's corporate man may indeed "carry a briefcase while pushing a baby carriage." And while he considers his career important, he goes to great effort not to sacrifice time with his family. His wife may have a demanding job, which he supports; but he may wonder if she thinks he's less of a man than her father, and he may resent her for the time she spends away from home.

In Kimmel's cultural analysis of manhood, he argues that a man's identity is largely taken from how he sees himself in the workplace. While at the turn of the nineteenth century, American manhood was rooted in land ownership or in being an independent artisan or farmer, the Industrial Revolution changed all that. And while the volatile marketplace was a far less stable venue for one's self-identity, it was certainly more exciting and potentially rewarding. Yet, as Kimmel notes, it did not deliver a peaceful existence:

> The Self-Made Man of American mythology was born anxious and insecure, uncoupled from the more stable anchors of landownership or workplace autonomy. Now manhood had to be proved. . . . This book is a history of the Self-Made Man—ambitious and anxious, creatively resourceful and chronically restive, the builder of culture and among the casualties of his own handiwork, a man who is, as the great French thinker Alexis de Tocqueville wrote in 1832, "restless in the midst of abundance."[3]

As the American male's idea of success has historically been tied to his financial success in the workplace, rooted in his autonomy and accomplishments, still he is "restless in the midst of abundance." Today's professional loves the deal, the chase, the game. Douglas LaBier describes *careerism* well when he states,

> Careerism has become the main work ethic of our times. At root, careerism is an attitude, a life orientation in which a person views [his or her] career as the primary and most important aim of life. An extreme but not uncommon expression of this is found in the comment of a man who told me that he feared dying mainly because it would mean the end of his career.[4]

LaBier's observation suggests that the modern professional does not fear death, but neither does he envision any overarching purpose as to why he works. His greatest fear of dying lies not in the traditional religious sentiments of guilt or possible judgment, but simply in the fact that when he dies he can no longer experience the euphoric experience of "making the deal." If pursued to its logical end, the mindset of careerism carries with it a certain malaise. Why? Because the business professional senses that nothing he or she does will have lasting significance.

A lot of my work is with business professionals, doing consulting, counseling and advising in the corporate arena. And I have always sensed this kind of despair as men look at their work, primarily, in purely temporal, materialistic terms. Job opportunities are evaluated almost exclusively on the financial rewards, with the hopes of building a nice retirement nest egg to enjoy "the rest" of his mortal days.

Sounds kind of short-term, wouldn't you say?

Work: Secular or Sacred?

This deep, abiding sense of the insignificance of work is the Achilles' heel of modernity. One can be successful, but what does it matter? Do these business meetings and daunting business trips accumulating rewards really make a difference? Does anything truly have an enduring value? Does anything in the workplace really matter? What's more, am I truly valued?

In his book *The Male Ego*, psychiatrist Willard Gaylin accurately captures the ambivalence and frustration of men, as illustrated by the following observation: "I have never met a man—among my patients or friends—who in his heart of hearts considers himself a success."

He satirizes the executive's need for "little pink roses," those pink message slips that tell a man that he's wanted. But when that chairman of the board or CEO finally retires, he suddenly learns he has lost all value. "He becomes a non-person," in Gaylin's words, shocked and overwhelmed by the fact that "he never was someone to be cherished for his own sake but only as an instrument of power and a conduit of goods."[5]

And I know from personal experience in working with men who have taken an early retirement that they desperately need the rush, the attention, the action of the workplace to feel a sense of dignity and worth. I remember advising one man who had left a successful medical practice to get back to work. His idle time around the house was driving his wife crazy.

Some would suggest that it is because work has been divorced from a transcendent perspective that we face such a crisis concerning our individual identity and significance. But someone may well ask, "What do you mean, transcendent dimension of work? How does my work have anything to do with something that lies beyond this world?" This question underscores the fact that modern culture sees little or no correlation between work and the issues of meaning and purpose. And when we view work only through the lens of a temporal life, it can easily lead to a despairing philosophy on life.

Leonard Woolf, the well-known British politician, made these candid observations years ago toward the end of his life:

> Looking back at the age of eighty-eight over the fifty-seven years of my political work in England, knowing what I aimed at and the results, . . . I see clearly that I achieved practically nothing. The world today and the history of the human ant hill during the last fifty-seven years would be exactly the same as it is if I had played ping pong instead of sitting on committees and writing books and memoranda. I have therefore to make the rather ignominious confession to myself and to anyone who may read this book that I must have in a long life ground through between 150,000 and 200,000 hours of perfectly useless work.[6]

A similar mindset to Woolf's still dominates the workplace today, and it is not far from the brutally frank observations we saw previously from the Preacher, Qoheleth, in his musings from the book of Ecclesiastes, where everything is a vapor, a vanity and a striving after wind.

There's always something more to pursue—another advancement to accept, another deal to close, another company to start and sell. One is reminded of novelist John Cheever's observation: "The main emotion of the adult American who has had all the advantages of wealth, education, and culture is disappointment."

Cheever, like a modern-day Solomon, put his finger on the pulse of the workplace. Even amid great financial and personal success, we remain ultimately unsatisfied and disenchanted. We want *more*. We even become bored and unfazed with great success, because it has come to be expected. And when work is divorced from a transcendent perspective, it can only be seen as futile, meaningless, vain and, yes, ultimately boring.

The great American playwright Arthur Miller, an astute observer of culture, called boredom "the hallmark of society as a whole," a society in which people merely exist and move among "a string of near-experiences marked off by periods of stupefying spiritual and psychological stasis, and the good life is basically an amazed one."

Work: Success or Significance?

Ultimate significance and satisfaction in work can be recognized only as we embrace what we have referenced as a sacramental perspective of life. Our work matters, and we celebrate our work, like the daily humdrum, because it signifies something more, transcendent matters.

Again, we may gain fame, fortune, prestige and power, but these signatures of success grow hollow and tinny if our work does not satisfy the deepest longings of our heart. Deep down, we want to know *why* we were placed on this earth. Our deepest passion is to know that we are fulfilling the purpose for which we were created. We need to have a sense of calling, to have a reason for our existence, to have a purpose, as Kierkegaard put it, "for which I can live and die."

And this deep down need for purpose is not just a contemporary phenomenon. In an early draft of the great Russian novelist Fyodor Dostoyevsky's *The Brothers Karamazov*, the Inquisitor gives a terrifying account of what happens to the human soul when it doubts its purpose: "For the secret of man's being is not only to live . . . but to live for something definite. Without a firm notion of what he is living for, man will not accept life and will rather destroy himself than remain on earth."[7] Without such an understanding, life is, as Shakespeare described it, "full of sound and fury, signifying nothing."

In his book *The Call: Finding and Fulfilling the Central Purpose of Your Life*, writer and Oxford theologian Os Guinness contends that we cannot divorce purpose and meaning in our work from a fundamentally religious view of life. He observes that people are looking not simply for success, but also for significance in life. This, too, is the premise of Bob Buford's best-selling book of a few years ago, *Halftime*, in which Buford contends that people spend the first half of their lives looking for *success* and the latter half looking for *significance*.

Recovering the Dignity of Work

While a secular view of work sees the purpose and goal of our labors here as simply temporal, without one overarching purpose, a more sacramental view sees our labors as a pointer to something more, something that will last. Such a sacramental view of life doesn't divide vocation and labor between

secular and sacred, but sees *all* of life as imbued with the transcendent. All work, like all of life, has inherent dignity. This
sacramental view of work has often been a central tenet of the
religious teachings of theologians and philosophers down
through the centuries.

The British writer Dorothy Sayers, writing in the mid-twentieth
century, chided the church on its neglect in formulating and
communicating a truly sacramental perspective on work. Sayers,
a gifted mystery writer and playwright, was a woman who passionately embraced her work as well as all of life.

Yet despite her passion for living, she found it difficult to
stick to her calling as a writer. Clergy often besieged her, re-
questing her to speak at garden *fêtes*, which would take her
away from her writing. She was also uncomfortable when fame
thrust her into the role of an apologist for Christianity as church
leaders sought to capitalize on her name. Yet she believed that
her vocation as a writer was deeply spiritual and that to be involved in anything less would have been to compromise her
own integrity and calling. She wrote passionately of the need for
a Christian theology of work that truly embraces a sacramental
view of all of life.

In an address she delivered in Eastbourne, England, entitled
"Why Work?" she lamented this failure of the organized church.

> In nothing has the Church so lost her hold on reality as in
> her failure to understand and respect the secular vocation.
> She has allowed work and religion to become separate de-
> partments, and is astonished to find that, as a result, the
> secular work of the world is turned to purely selfish and
> destructive ends, and that the greater part of the world's
> intelligent workers have become irreligious, or at least,
> uninterested in religion. But is it astonishing? How can

any one remain interested in a religion which seems to have no concern with nine-tenths of his life?[8]

Sayers rightly understood that work should not be divorced from a transcendent perspective of life. A true grasp of reality sees an inseparable connection between our work and who we are as individuals and what ultimately matters to us.

Pursuing Excellence in Work

What is it that makes us pursue excellence in our work? Why do we appreciate and admire a job well done? Certainly all societies of all ages have admired "quality" work, whether it's in the sales force, in the laboratory, as a financial manager or on the athletic field.

The Shakers have become synonymous with excellence. Each Shaker chair, it was said, was to be of high enough quality for an angel to sit on. Shakers were to make every product better than it had been made before, including not only the parts they could see but also the parts they couldn't. They were to use only the best materials, even for the most everyday items, and were advised to give attention to the smallest of details. Everything was to be designed and made as if it would last forever.

C. S. Lewis reminds us that, unfortunately, the work of the saints has sometimes lacked this standard of excellence with which we have been provided. In his essay "Good Work and Good Works" he wrote,

> "Good works" in the plural is an expression much more familiar to modern Christendom than "good work." . . . And good works need not be good work, as anyone can see by inspecting some of the objects made to be sold at bazaars for charitable purposes. This is not according to our example. When our Lord provided a poor wedding party

with an extra glass of wine all round, he was doing good
works. But also good work; it was a wine really worth
drinking. . . . Let choirs sing well or not at all.[9]

Lewis was right: let the choir sing well, or let them be silent.
While a lot of religious institutions are known for their work of
excellence, too many are known for shoddy work that they
deem acceptable because it is done in the name of God. Interestingly, the essence of this quest for excellence is captured by
the plaque beside Sayers's gravesite, which summarizes her
philosophy of living: "The only Christian work is a good work
well done."

Those thoughtful Christians from an earlier time knew intui-
tively that our work matters and should be pursued with excellence, because it will last, and it points to another world that
awaits us.

How Does Work Fulfill Us?

In his best-selling book *If Aristotle Ran General Motors*, Tom
Morris, a former philosophy professor at Notre Dame, draws on
the wisdom of history's wisest thinkers to demonstrate their
contribution to the contemporary workplace. Addressing the
present challenges in the workplace environment, he observes
that for quite some time American business leaders have been
talking about rediscovering the vital importance of product and
service quality in our highly competitive world.

In recent years, nearly everyone has been talking about re-
engineering the corporation and redesigning the processes by
which work is done to attain greater efficiencies and new forms
of business excellence. While management strategies have mul-
tiplied, we've become inundated with new techniques and find
ourselves almost drowning in information. For all the bally-

hooed talk about excellence in the workplace, something very important has been forgotten, as Morris observes:

> Behind the products, services, and processes of modern business, behind all the strategies and techniques and data, are the people who do the work. And too often . . . the employees of modern businesses feel themselves more the victims than the beneficiaries of the new corporate strategies for success. . . . Too many people feel insecure, threatened, and unappreciated in their jobs. . . . People at work are the only true foundation for lasting excellence, and so I think the time has come to focus on the deeply human issues of happiness, satisfaction, meaning, and fulfillment in the workplace.[10]

The CEOs and other business leaders that I have had the opportunity to meet and work with over the years have always had this sense of the importance of the dignity of the individual. True, they value their employees' excellent work, but they also care for them as individuals.

And genuine, fulfilling happiness is experienced when we are significantly involved in a job or career that we think is important. Getting rewarded for work well done is important to us, but it's not the sole reason we work or the sole motivation. Even the great Walt Disney realized that happiness in life was more than the accumulation of wealth. He observed,

> I've always been bored with just making money. I've wanted to do things, I wanted to build things. Get something going. . . . I'm not like some people who worship money as something you've got to have piled up in a big pile somewhere. I've only thought of money in one way, and that is to do something with it. . . . I don't think there

is a thing that I own that I will ever get the benefit of, except through doing things with it.[11]

Disney's words and approach to living suggest that happiness is a dynamic phenomenon of participation in something that brings fulfillment. This was beautifully portrayed in the film *Chariots of Fire*, when Eric Liddell proclaims that God has made him to run fast, "and when I run, I feel His pleasure." And I love the sage advice of novelist Frederick Buechner, who suggests that "the place God calls you to is the place where your deep gladness and the world's deep hunger meet."[12]

Truly, one of the greatest expressions of our humanness in this drama called life is our satisfying engagement in a job worth doing. There is a dignity and worth to all work, and when we are participants in a worthwhile task, it results in genuine fulfillment and happiness. We know that exclusively pursuing pleasure—the mere accumulation of wealth, fame and fortune—does not bring genuine happiness. Deep down we want more than money and recognition.

We enjoy our times of vacation, rest and relaxation, but *work* is part of our living, and we crave the hustle and bustle. We want activity and we want to work. When we stop working, we lose touch with an important aspect of our humanity.

Have you noticed how bored wealthy or retired people often become when they stop working, even though they may have ample financial resources? I've often advised professional men who have retired early to reenter the marketplace with the remarkable skills they possess, because their contribution can be considerable and because work brings significant satisfaction to their lives.

When we begin to understand the transcendent nature of work, we see it in a new light. Our work points beyond ourselves—and our world— maybe to an earlier time, perhaps to a sort of edenic experience, when things were pure and unspoiled. And somehow, in ways that we cannot fully comprehend, that connection is still there. Perhaps the significance and joy we get from good work is a harbinger of another world that awaits us.

- 7 -

Leisure and Play

Looking for Paradise?

*Baseball is our religion. The stadium's our temple.
The beer and peanuts, our sacrament.*

ADVERTISEMENT IN *USA TODAY*

*Most middle-class Americans tend to
worship their work, to work at their play, and to
play at their worship. As a result, their meanings and values
are distorted. Their relationships disintegrate faster than they
can keep them in repair, and their lifestyles resemble
a cast of characters in search of a plot.*

**GORDON DAHL, *WORK, PLAY, AND WORSHIP
IN A LEISURE-ORIENTED SOCIETY***

As we saw in the previous chapter, we Americans are passionate about our work. As part of our celebrated Puritan work ethic, work continues to have a prominent place in the American psyche. Yet, as the Gordon Dahl quote above suggests, we are still seeking to restore balance between our work and leisure time.

We are discovering the importance of creating lasting memories with our families and friends. Whether it is in the mountains, on the coast, on the tennis courts, on the golf course or while watching a football or baseball game, we want leisure and play. But a question remains that is rarely addressed: What exactly is leisure, anyway? Is it the same thing as "play"? What is the true meaning and purpose of leisure? What are we supposed to do with leisure time? What do we even mean by *leisure*?

What Is Leisure?

To most of us, leisure has an ethereal feel to it, like smoke through our fingers. The concept of leisure may create hazy associations, even of boredom. And while postcards and glossy advertisements lure us to faraway place for "R and R," the nature and essence of true leisure still eludes us. In truth, we often come back from vacations worn out, in need of rest.

Part of our dilemma stems from the various synonyms used to describe leisure, such as *play*, *game* and *recreation*. Further complicating our understanding, some define leisure as an activity, while others describe it as a state of mind. While our modern culture tends to conceive of leisure as our "free time"— that time not devoted to our paid vocations—the older, classical tradition conceives of leisure as the cultivation of the self and a preoccupation with the higher virtues of life.

How different our idea of leisure is today amid a compulsively utilitarian culture that measures virtually everything we do through the lens of work. We even speak of "playing" or "going on vacation" so that we can come back refreshed and ready to be more productive *in our jobs*. Is the idea of a "working vacation" not a contradiction in terms?

Leisure: A Celebration of Life

The true sense of genuine leisure and play, while certainly being set apart from our "work lives," includes much more. While it involves a break from the tedium and monotony of the everyday, it also carries with it the idea of contemplation and celebration of the world we inhabit. Commenting on the distinctiveness of leisure, Josef Pieper observes,

> Leisure does not mean the same as a "break." . . . Leisure is something entirely different. The essence of leisure is not to assure that we may function smoothly but rather to assure that we, embedded in our social function, are enabled to remain fully human. . . . That we may . . . contemplate and celebrate the world as such, to become and be that person who is essentially oriented toward the whole of reality.[1]

True leisure, then, is self-reflective in nature and helps us to better understand the world and ourselves. Leisure leads us to ask ourselves some deep and penetrating questions about who we are, what we are doing and where we are going.

And perhaps more than any other time in our history, we need to learn anew how to give ourselves permission to reflect on our lives as well as to relax and enjoy life. Even King Solomon, three thousand years ago, penned these words about the importance of taking time to reflect on the goodness of life and on the vast richness of the human experience.

> Go then, eat your bread in happiness, and drink your wine with a cheerful heart; for God has already approved your works. . . . Enjoy life with the woman whom you love all the days of your fleeting life which He has given to you under the sun; for this is your reward in life and in your toil in which you have labored under the sun. (Ecclesiastes 9:7, 9)

To live life with gaiety and frivolity, then, is certainly not frivolous. It is a celebration of our humanness, our proclaiming that the world is good. And when we reflect on the many blessings of life, it often leads to deeper contemplation. We cannot overestimate the importance of noticing the "small things" in life and listening to our lives. This is part of genuine leisure and contemplation.

The renowned architect Frank Lloyd Wright once told of an incident that perhaps seemed insignificant at the time, but had a profound influence on the rest of his life. The winter he was nine years old, he went walking across a snow-covered field with his reserved, no-nonsense uncle. As the two of them reached the far end of the field, his uncle stopped him and pointed out his own tracks in the snow, straight and true as an arrow's flight. He then pointed out young Frank's tracks, which meandered all over the field. "Notice how your tracks wander aimlessly from the fence to the cattle to the woods and back again," his uncle said. "And see how my tracks aim directly to my goal. There is an important lesson in that." Years later, Wright liked to tell how this experience greatly contributed to his philosophy of life. "I determined right then," he said with a twinkle in his eye, "not to miss most things in life, as my uncle had."

I think Wright's meandering across that snow-covered field, curiously looking at everything in his path, comes very close to this notion of contemplation and genuine leisure. In our times of festivity and leisure, we sense the grandeur and beauty of the world. And when we make time for leisure and play, such rest becomes not simply a break in the monotony of daily living, but rather a celebration of life itself. And our souls come away refreshed from the experience.

I recall years ago camping in the collegiate peaks of Colorado, some 12,000 to 14,000 feet above sea level. I got above the timberline and saw the beauty of snow-covered mountains and of mountain lilies. At nighttime, so far away from the lights of the city, the stars were literally bursting in the dark skies, too innumerable to count. Nature teaches us a lot about life, if we will listen.

Throughout history philosophers have reflected on the nature of leisure and play, and have sensed a transcendent, spiritual dimension to leisure and sport. This has come about as they have observed humans through the centuries absorbed in the act of playing or being spectators in a human drama to see how a game "plays out." Aristotle was a key contributor to this mindset and believed that in play, humankind comes closest to genuine contemplation.

In some of our most cherished sports, there are what have come to be called "signals of transcendence." Leisure and sports therefore signal to us another world to come. Let's consider two sports that whet our appetite for the Something More: golf, which Mark Twain called "a good walk spoiled," and baseball, that good old American pastime.

Golf: A Good Walk Spoiled?

If you've ever played golf, I'm sure you would agree with me that it has to be one of the most frustrating sports ever concocted. My buddies and I play frequently, in virtually any kind of weather. And for all the pleasure of hitting those shots that keep us coming back for more, it is still a terribly frustrating sport. Even guys on the PGA tour become exasperated by their poor shots, which are quite rare.

Golfers are known to frequently vent their frustrations to friends and are often met with the puzzled question from spouses and friends, "If you love golf so much, why are you so upset after playing a round?" John Feinstein, the award-winning sports writer, begins his enjoyable book *A Good Walk Spoiled: Days and Nights on the PGA Tour* with the Twain phrase in his title, highlighting the mysterious conundrum about golf.

Along similar lines, celebrated psychiatrist M. Scott Peck, author of *The Road Less Traveled*, declares in his book *Golf and the Spirit* that golf is "probably the most nonlinear pastime on the face of the earth." Consequently, he sees an important lesson played out in the game of golf: most of the time, life and reality do not behave the way we want them to.[2]

In many ways, golf is the least precise game in the world; golfers rarely are able to determine with any precision exactly *why* they are playing well or poorly. Without fail, even when someone is playing well—in "the zone"—he waits with trepidation for the "wheels to come off." He knows that it's just a matter of time before he will lose the rhythm and confidence that allowed him to "master" the past few holes.

Even among the best golf professionals, there are no surefire answers for improving one's game. Just take a look at all the bulging instructional sections in golf magazines; golfers are all looking for the secret that doesn't exist. On the severity of the game, Feinstein observes,

> No one has the answers. . . . Hard work can make you better but it won't always make you better. Sometimes, it will make you worse. Golf has no guarantees. And what makes it even more difficult, there are no excuses. . . . No one ever gets a bad call in golf. No one strikes you out or tackles you or blocks your shot or hits a forehand so hard you can't get to it. The ball doesn't move and neither does the hole. You either get the ball into the hole quickly or not quickly enough. Period. . . . There is no sport as solitary as golf. No sport humanizes you like golf.[3]

Golf keeps track of every mistake. Unlike many sports, where one can make a comeback to get back in the game, there are no second chances with golf. In tennis, which is frequently compared to golf because both are individual sports, you can fall behind two sets but rally to win. In golf, every shot counts. Every mistake is deftly recorded on a scorecard—and in ink. PGA professional Billy Andrade, a friend to many major league baseball players, enjoys telling them, "You can strike out your first three times up and still be a hero by hitting a homer your fourth time up. In golf, you make three errors and you're dead." Or as the legendary Sam Snead once chided Hall of Famer Ted Williams, "In golf, you have to play your foul balls."[4]

In golf, we learn a lot about ourselves, about who we really are. Walker Percy often uses the golf course as a setting reminiscent of his childhood memories of growing up in the suburbs of Birmingham, Alabama. To him, golf is a remarkable contemplative sport that fosters self-understanding, understanding of this world and understanding of others.

In Percy's novel *The Second Coming*, the central character is Will Barrett, a successful middle-aged attorney who is despairing and bored with life. Barrett firmly believes that someone can learn more about a man from playing a round of golf with him than could be learned from spending a year of sessions on a psychiatrist's couch. In his excellent biography of Percy, *Pilgrim in the Ruins*, Jay Tolson makes this interesting observation about Percy and his penchant for including golf in his works:

> The triumph of golf in the South is itself a curious fact of cultural history. It is, as anyone who has ever played it knows, a penitential little game, as much a trial of character and bearing as of skill. (Walker Percy . . . would later explore the peculiar moral dimensions of the game in

almost as much depth as his northern fellow-in-letters, John Updike.) Fittingly, golf was invented by a Scotsman, for only a Calvinist could have found pleasure in a pursuit that required so much restraint for so delayed a reward.[5]

In many ways, golf serves as a metaphor for life. And if golf teaches us anything, it mercilessly shows us our failures and shortcomings in life. While in many avenues of life we may attempt to fool ourselves or others into thinking that we are doing wonderfully, golf is not nearly so kind and forgiving. Golf gives us a glimpse of our inner souls. John Updike's essay "Moral Exercise" vividly describes the brutal honesty of the game:

> Most of us don't really know how well we're doing, in real life, and imagine we're doing not so bad. The world conspires to flatter us; only golf trusts us with a cruelly honest report on our performance. Only on the golf course is the feedback instantaneous and unrelenting. . . . In the sound of the hit and the flight of the ball it tells us unflinchingly how we are doing, and we are rarely doing well.[6]

Golf testifies, as Updike suggests, that we are imperfect creatures. Yet for some odd reason, many of us are drawn to the game, perhaps because we are seeking perfection, or at least the perfect swing or shot.

A similar scenario is beautifully portrayed in Michael Murphy's best-selling book *Golf in the Kingdom.* It's the imaginary story of a young man en route to India who stops in Scotland to play the legendary Burningbush Golf Club, where his life is transformed. The young man is paired with a mysterious club professional named Shivas Irons, who leads him through a phenomenal round of golf. Murphy's book, laden with a good dose of Eastern mysticism, provides some interesting insight into the game, particularly in the provocative chapter entitled "A Hamartiology of Golf." The chapter describes how a faulty golf swing reflects the soul and, more particularly, our "coming up short" in our moral character.

> Peter McNaughton had remarked that nowhere does a man go so naked as he does before a discerning eye all dressed for golf. Shivas recalled the remark and asked me if I knew the word "hamartia." "It originally meant bein' off the target, in archery or some such," he said, "and then it came to mean bein' off the taraget in general in all yer life—it got to mean a flaw in the character. . . . When a man swings he tells us all about himself." . . . "Yes, a man's style o' play and his swing certainly reflect the state of his soul," he resumed his description of golfing hamartiology, "Ye take the one who always underclub. The man who wants to think he's stronger than he is. D' ye ken anybody like that?" He raised one quizzical eyebrow. "Think about the rest of his habits. Is he always short o' the hole?"[7]

Despite abysmal failures on the course, golfers often go to extreme measures to correct flawed, aggressive swings and wayward putting strokes. In how many other sports do you see professional athletes going out to practice for hours after they've played for the day?

Most golfers love working at their game and realize that they will fail more often than they succeed. Citing this curious aspect of golf, Greg Norman observed, "The failure is what makes succeeding so sweet. . . . In golf, failure is a great thing—an absolutely necessary thing." Failure teaches us a lot about life and a lot about ourselves. It reveals our deeply flawed character.

Golf seems to go beyond being a metaphor, since it reveals what we are really like deep inside. Golf is the ultimate head and heart game. To play golf is a spiritual exercise, because it deflates our ego and shows us how far we have to go.

I've always appreciated the response of Scott Peck to the question of why he persists in playing golf, even though he is regularly confronted with his shortcomings. He candidly remarked,

> I play golf precisely because it is humiliating. While I don't enjoy being humiliated, I do need it. There's another word for what golfers go through that's even stronger than humiliation: mortification. It is derived from *mors*, the Latin word for "death," as is the term mortician for "undertaker." To be mortified is to feel so humiliated that you would rather bury yourself deep in the nearest sand trap than ever show your face on a golf course again. . . . In doing battle on the golf course against my own personality—against my ego, if you will—I am attempting to practice kenosis: getting myself out of my own way. It is what spiritual growth is all about. . . . Among other reasons, I play golf because it is for me a highly useful spiritual discipline.[8]

To be honest, neither I nor most of the guys I have played golf with over the years look at it as a "spiritual exercise," telling us about our inner soul and our need for improvement. But just maybe it serves that kind of function. Golf keeps score, and none of us are doing really that well.

And despite the frustrating things about the game, I've got to say that the camaraderie I've experienced on the links with a group of guys—whether it was at our local club or such unbelievable destinations as Pebble Beach, St. Andrews or Newport Golf Club in Newport, Rhode Island—are filled with wonderful memories that make life worth living.

But in addition to showing our imperfections and allowing us to bask in the wonders of nature, golf teaches something about life itself, if you will. In golf we come to understand that the game is played not so much by might as it is by feeling that appropriate rhythm where grace and freedom abound. We who play the game know that the worst thing in the world for a golf swing is to be tense or to attempt to muscle that little white ball down the open fairway.

Hopefully, we can occasionally relax and enjoy that "saintly" letting go that golf asks of its devotees. And in the process, we might gain a bit more insight into what it means to live by faith. John Updike says it so well:

> Unreconstituted Adam wants to kill the ball, and to watch it fly. . . . The correct golf swing is a web of small articles of faith, all of which strain common sense. . . . Taking a light grip goes dead against our furious determination to hammer the course into submission. . . . Golf is a study in our greed as well as our lack of faith. In remembering a round, we write off the missed two-foot putt and the approach shot that just barely drifted into the trap as not us, as not legitimately part of the round, but incorporate without gratitude the skulled wedge that somehow wound up on the green.[9]

Baseball: The Great American Pastime

In addition to golf, while many would argue that college and professional football have replaced baseball as America's favorite pastime, baseball remains a game for reflection and contemplation as it relates to leisure and to thoughts of transcendence in our world. For many of us, baseball *matters*, and it signifies something more than the game itself. Baseball resonates deeply within us, probably more than any other sport in the American culture.

Ken Burns, the producer and director of the popular PBS

series *Baseball*, expressed this sentiment in a speech before the National Press Club in Washington, D.C., a few years ago: "Baseball is a Rosetta Stone upon which you can see writ quite plainly the soul of the country."

While some people look at all sports as mere escapism, akin to double-strength Tylenol—harmless enough, but certainly distracting us from the real issues of life—in the classical perspective, sports were not viewed as an elixir for escapism. Rather, sports were perceived to deal with the contemplation of the higher values of life. George Will, in his critically acclaimed book *Men at Work: The Craft of Baseball*, comments on the classic understanding of sports as it relates to baseball:

> Proof of the genius of ancient Greece is that it understood baseball's future importance. . . . Sport, they said, is morally serious because mankind's noblest aim is the loving contemplation of worthy things, such as beauty and courage. . . . Seeing people compete courageously and fairly helps emancipate the individual by educating his passions.[10]

It seems that in the game of baseball, not only do we experience the high drama of winning or losing, we also yearn for what is best in ourselves. We become spectators, not for any selfish reasons such as fame or fortune (maybe this is the reason for the public's disdain for selfish players and owners), but simply because the game is there, and we lose ourselves in the game being played out.

Years ago songwriter and longtime Yankees fan Paul Simon was asked to explain his appeal to Joe DiMaggio in the song "Mrs. Robinson." He replied, "It has something to do with *heroes* . . . people who are all good with no bad in them. That's the way I always saw Joe DiMaggio."

In addition to the high drama and our aspiration for worthy heroes, baseball serves as a metaphor for justice and right-eousness. It appeals to our deep moral sense of how things *ought* to be. Baseball attempts to provide a level playing field of what life should be like. And as we attempt to sort out the rhythms and reasons of life, through baseball we seek to ensure a *predictable* outcome that is often lacking in the drama of real life. What else could account for the insatiable keeping of statistics?

Our deep longing for fairness is poignantly expressed in the words of Thomas Boswell, the renowned writer for the *Washington Post*, in his classic on baseball, *Why Time Begins on Opening Day*:

> In contrast to the unwieldy world which we hold in common, baseball offers a kingdom built to human scale. Its problems and questions are exactly our size. Here we come when we feel a need for a rooted point of reference. . . . Baseball isn't necessarily an escape from reality, though it can be; it's merely one of our many refuges within the real where we try to create a sense of order on our own terms. Born to an age where horror has become common-place, where tragedy has, by its monotonous repetition, become a parody of sorrow, we need to fence off a few parks where humans try to be fair, where skill has some hope of reward, where absurdity has a harder time than usual getting a ticket.[11]

But perhaps even greater than our desire for justice and fairness on the playing field, the baseball diamond signifies our aspirations for some sort of paradise. While there is little that can compare with the excitement of the World Series each fall, by the same token, each spring, baseball ushers in a season of promise and hope—not just on the field, but beyond the fence—

through the prism of our lives going into the "late innings."

Bartlett Giamatti, who taught Renaissance literature at Yale and served as baseball's seventh commissioner until his untimely death, was fond of pointing out the similarities between the contemporary and ancient worlds. He noted that the etymological root for the word *paradise* is an ancient Persian word meaning "enclosed park or green." Baseball, Giamatti suggested, inspires us toward deep and resonant hopes and reminds us of a time of innocence, another world.

> So much does our game tell us about what we wanted to be, about what we are. Our character and our culture are reflected in this grand game. It would be foolish to think that all of our national experience is reflected in any single institution, even our loftiest, but it would not be wrong to claim for baseball a capacity to cherish individuality and inspire cohesion in a way which is a hallmark of our loftiest free institutions. Nor would it be misguided to think that, however vestigial the remnants of our best hopes, we can still find, if we wish to, a moment called a game when those best hopes, those memories for the future, have life; when each of us, those who are in and those out, has a chance to gather, in a green place around home.[12]

Sports: Looking for Paradise?

As we have seen regarding golf and baseball, we enjoy them not only for providing a break from the hurried pace of life, but also for providing a window to our souls.

Golf provides a case study of what kind of people we really are and serves as a spiritual exercise in humility and mortification, as Peck and Updike remind us. Our golf swing shows us unapologetically how far we have fallen short of perfection.

And in baseball, we experience the high drama of winning or losing, and we look for fairness and justice on the playing field, something that cannot be counted on in the game of life. Furthermore, in baseball, we look beyond the "enclosed park or green," a signpost to another time, where our dreams and aspirations may one day be realized.

When you think about the sports that you are fond of—whether it is golf or baseball, tennis or fly-fishing, or spectator sports such as football or soccer—do you deep down believe they signify much more than the game itself?

Amid the trials and pains that we experience in this life, this veil of tears and tribulation, leisure—especially as seen in contemplative sports—possibly provides a respite from this world. Beneath the veneer of life, sports may actually image an abiding joy that will one day be the serious business of another world.

Transcendence in Literature and Film

Why should a man be scorned, if,
finding himself in prison, he tries to get out and go home?
Or if, when he cannot do so, he thinks and talks about other topics than
jailers and prison-walls? The world outside has not become
less real because the prisoner cannot see it.

J. R. R. TOLKIEN, *ON FAIRY—STORIES*

Behind the corpse in the reservoir, behind the ghost on the links,
Behind the lady who dances and the man who madly drinks,
Under the look of fatigue, the attack of migraine and the sigh
There is always another story, there is more than meets the eye.

W. H. AUDEN

Yet another pointer in our experience that we may be created for another world involves the sense of transcendence, or of the numinous, that we observe in the arts, particularly through literature and the cinema.

What do we mean by the sense of the numinous? It might

best be understood as seeing this present life as almost haunted by something that, although invisible, is nevertheless a real presence. And this sense of the numinous pervades all of our experience and inspires fear and awe in us, though we are unable to define or articulate precisely what we mean by it. We only know that we meet this sense of the numinous in the strangest of ways: in films, plays, literature, art and music.

Art moves us and touches something deep within our souls. Who can remain unmoved when observing some of the world's great works of art? We are taken outside of ourselves. Anyone that visits the British Museum in London or the Louvre in Paris, with its collection of over thirty thousand works of art (including the works of Raphael, Da Vinci and Van Gogh), most definitely comes away with a sense of awe and transcendence.

Or reflect for a moment on how music moves us. I vividly remember years ago attending an evensong service at Christ Church Cathedral in Oxford. As the boys choir chanted inside this exquisite Oxford cathedral, it was a transcendent moment of worship that I will never forget. Perhaps this helps explain why the ancients ascribed music to the gods, the muses. No, music is more than aesthetic pleasure, and some would suggest that it is a divine haunting that signifies God's presence in the world. Some have suggested that if there is a Bach, there must definitely be a God.[1]

Listen to how the great conductor Leonard Bernstein described the effect of Beethoven on him:

> Beethoven . . . turned out pieces of breath-taking rightness. Rightness—that's the word! When you get the feeling that whatever note succeeds the last is the only possible note that can rightly happen at that instant, in that context, then chances are you're listening to Beethoven. . . . Our

boy has the real goods, the stuff of Heaven, the power to make you feel at the finish: Something is right in the world. There is something that checks throughout, that follows its own law consistently: something we can trust, that will never let us down.[2]

In contrast to Bernstein's observations about Beethoven, a merely physical world stripped of its grandeur and awe would be the mere product of an exclusively materialistic universe: without mystery or strangeness. Yet such a view of life doesn't feed the soul, as Bernstein suggests about the works of Beethoven.

What's more, this sense of the numinous that we encounter in art is the basis of tales and myths that often are populated by elves, fairies, wizards, dragons, even gods and goddesses. Some suggest that it is this deep-rooted sense of the numinous, the sacramental, that inspires wonder, awe and worship. One would have a difficult time underestimating the power and sense of mystery that accompanies Tolkien's Lord of the Rings trilogy, under the direction of master filmmaker Peter Jackson, that made its way to the cinema in the past decade.

While we could consider a multitude of various genres of art, we will confine our discussion in this chapter to a brief consideration of literature and film. As we will see, the great writers and filmmakers who have influenced and continue to influence our culture are imbued with notions of transcendence. Whatever the medium, art reflects the soul of a culture. Novelist Marcel Proust once observed that "through art we can know another's view of the universe."

Literature: Writers and the Notion of Transcendence

While we can only briefly consider the hint of transcendence within literature, we need to first realize that many writers have a gripe with God. What one observes in the American literary landscape is a preoccupation—almost obsession—with God and any notion of an afterlife.

Alfred Kazin writes of this quest for something akin to faith on the part of these writers in his much-heralded book *God and the American Writer*. He devotes a chapter to some of the most celebrated of America's twentieth-century writers: Hawthorne, Emerson, Stowe, Melville, Whitman, Lincoln, Dickinson, James, Twain, Eliot, Frost and Faulkner. He presents not so much their personal profession of belief, but rather their "quarreling with God," because they were frequently at odds with their orthodox Christian heritage. Their mindset is aptly displayed in a quote from Emily Dickinson found in the prelude to the book: "We thank thee, Father, for these strange minds that enamor us against thee."

Interestingly, Kazin omitted John Updike from his book, whose writings have mirrored his continual quest to understand the place of God in our world. And yet Updike displays a curious religious thinking on the role of faith and the religious impulse. He amusingly referred to himself as a token "Christian" contributor when he was a part of the *New Yorker* staff. When he received the Campion Medal in honor of the brilliant Jesuit theologian St. Edmund Campion in September of 1997 in New York City, he made these remarks about the role of faith in his writing:

> It is all too easy a thing to be a Christian in America, where God's name is on our coinage, pious pronouncements are routinely expected from elected officials, and churchgoing, though far from unanimous, enjoys a popularity astounding to Europeans. . . . Yes, I have been a churchgoer in three Protestant denominations—Lutheran, Congrega-

tional, Episcopal—and the Christian faith has given me comfort in my life and, I would like to think, courage in my work. For it tells us that truth is holy, and truth-telling a noble and useful profession; that the reality around us is created and worth celebrating; that men and women are radically imperfect and radically valuable.[3]

The Literary Classics: What Does It Mean to Be Human?

We often encounter a sense of the transcendent when we read the great classics of literature, because they transport us to other worlds, times and places. While reading in our culture is sometimes considered a lost or dying art due to the proliferation of the visual and technological media, the classics keep us in touch with the past.

In great literature, not only are we challenged to know the past, but we are also inspired to live in the present and future. The classics have a way of pointing beyond the immediate and the ordinary to another world. There is something almost magical about getting into a good novel that has interesting characters and an intriguing plot.

In many ways, stories have a way of drawing us into their world. We come to appreciate through the joys and travails of characters what it is to be a part of the human drama. American playwright Arthur Miller, author of *The Death of a Salesman*, when asked how he knew he had discovered a great script, said it was when he found himself saying of the characters, "My God, that's me!" Perhaps one of the central elements behind great literature is that it transcends the immediate and applies to the universal human condition. In a way, good literature mirrors real life.

Some would suggest that the classics of Western civilization have withstood the test of time because they grapple with these universal issues of humanity: What does it mean to live life? How do I achieve significance and purpose in this present life? What happens at death? Is there life after death? The classics carry the scent of transcendence.

Over the years I've been involved in various reading groups, most of which have focused on literary classics. The amazing thing that we have discovered as we have read such works is how current they are to the issues we face every day. Even though many are hundreds of years old, they speak to the universal human condition and often about our human search for God, meaning and purpose.

What's more, many of the Western civilization classics are fundamentally based on a Christian worldview of life. Reynolds Price, the late author and professor of English at Duke University, wrote of his abiding belief in orthodox Christianity as reflected in the Apostles' Creed. Price, who acknowledged that such a creed may be stated but not "defended with a satisfying dossier of empirical evidence," concluded,

> The final help I can offer the proof-hungry is a reminder that virtually identical beliefs powered perhaps a majority of the supreme creative minds of our civilization— Augustine, Dante, Chaucer, Michelangelo, Durer, Milton, Rembrandt, Pascal, Racine, Bach, Handel, Newton, Haydn, Mozart, Wordsworth, Beethoven, Kierkegaard, Dickens, Tolstoy . . . Auden, O'Connor (to begin a long roll that includes only the dead). Pressed by their unanimous testimony to a dazzling but benign light at the heart of space, what sane human will step up to say "Lovely, no doubt, but your eyes deceive you"? Not I, not now or any day soon.[4]

The Enchanted World of Fairy Tales

While the classics of Western civilization continue to have an enduring legacy, telling us what it means to be human, it's in fairy tales that we frequently encounter a sense of awe, wonder and enchantment with this world.

Memorable are the magical worlds of Kenneth Graham's *The Wind in the Willows*, J. R. R. Tolkien's *The Hobbit* and the Lord of the Rings trilogy, and C. S. Lewis's Chronicles of Narnia. While some critics may suggest that fairy tales are only for children, giving a false impression of the world, Lewis wrote,

> I think no literature children could read gives them less of a false impression. . . . It would be much truer to say that fairyland arouses a longing for he knows not what. It stirs . . . him (to his life-long enrichment) with the dim sense of something beyond his reach and, far from dulling the actual world, . . . gives it a new dimension of depth. He does not despise real woods because he has read of enchanted woods: the reading makes all real woods a little enchanted.[5]

When we look at the world through the window of the fairy tale, we are met with astonishment and awe, and we find a heightened sense of the numinous, the haunting of this world, which points us toward another world. Tolkien, Lewis's literary companion in the Oxford gathering known as the Inklings, once declared, "If the story succeeds, you look out of it; if it fails, you look *into* it."[6]

Therefore, both the literary classics and fairy tales not only instruct us about what it means to be human, but also suggest to us another world that lies beyond this temporal, visible world. Even the phenomenal successes of the recent *Harry Potter* series by J. K. Rowling and Tolkien's Lord of the Rings trilogy can be attributed not just to the fact that the stories tell a good yarn, but also that they tap into the longing most of us feel for that better, magic-filled world.

When we trudge up a dusty hill with Frodo and Samwise in Tolkien's Middle Earth or explore the enchanted world of Lewis's Narnia with the Pevensie children, where the "inside is bigger than the outside," or when we fly in a purple car with Harry Potter and his friends, our present experience of pain and sorrow is diminished and our longings for another world become more real.

Transcendence in Film

Some would suggest that the influence of literature has waned significantly since the days of Tolstoy or Dostoyevsky. With the decline in reading skills that many have dated starting in the late 1960s, some studies have suggested that only slightly over half of all Americans spend thirty minutes a day reading anything at all.

Indeed, in our media-frenzied culture of iPads, iPhones and laptops that surf the Internet via Wi-Fi hotspots, the visual feast presented through the cinema may be one of the last cultural experiences shared by a majority of Americans. What's more, even more Americans are turning to create their own "home theater" experiences with the proliferation of media options that are now available to the average consumer, or they are choosing to watch media on their phones or iPads.

That film has largely replaced the novel as the dominant mode of artistic expression is undeniable for the general public, who increasingly tend to be more image than word oriented. Some movie critics and scholars have even gone so far as to suggest that movies are permeating our culture with a new paradigm for comprehending reality.

Whatever opinion we may have on the superiority of film to

literary art, it's important to our discussion that filmmaking, like all art, is often preoccupied with *transcendent* questions about what may lie beyond this temporal life. Some of the most influential directors and filmmakers in the history of cinema have been unabashedly preoccupied with the spiritual dimension to life. Let's look at a few of these filmmakers.

Martin Scorsese. Over the past few decades, Scorsese is one of the most passionate and inventive filmmakers. His work is often rooted in his own background, as he explores his Italian-American Catholic heritage and regularly confronts the themes of sin and redemption in his works, albeit in a contemporary fashion. Scorsese is best known for *Taxi Driver* (1976), *Raging Bull* (1980), *Goodfellas* (1990) and *Cape Fear* (1991), which all include his good friend Robert De Niro, who also grew up in New York's Little Italy.

More recently, Scorsese's second Golden Globe Award for best director came for his work in *The Departed* (2006), the Boston-set thriller—based on the Hong Kong police drama *Internal Affairs*—which starred Leonardo DiCaprio and Jack Nicholson. The film follows the overlapping careers of Billy (Leonardo DiCaprio) and Colin (Matt Damon). Both go undercover and play a character for a larger mission, yet in Scorsese's nihilistic world, all the characters face a bloody end.

The Departed accurately demonstrates the grim consequences of a world where God is absent. It is a dark and brooding cinematic story about hearts of darkness, where a very thin line separates the cops from the criminals, and through the will to power, man must master his own universe. It opens with Frank Costello (Jack Nicholson) dispensing some heady advice:

> I don't want to be a product of my environment. I want my environment to be a product of me. Years ago we had the

church. That was only a way of saying—we had each other.
. . . Church wants you in your place. Kneel, stand, kneel,
stand. If you go for that sort of thing. I don't know what to
do for you. A man has to make his own way. No one gives
it to you. You have to take it.[7]

Ironically, as a misbehaving class clown at a Catholic high
school, Scorsese dreamed of becoming a priest. He went so far as
to study briefly at Cathedral College, a junior Catholic seminary.
Yet rather than devote himself entirely to the church, he enrolled
in New York University and soon discovered that film could
serve as a tremendous vehicle for his own transcendent musings
on life. In response to the criticism he received for the film *The
Last Temptation of Christ* (1986), Scorsese shot back, "My whole
life has been movies and religion. That's it. Nothing else."[8]

In a book based on a BBC documentary, *A Personal Journey
with Martin Scorsese Through American Movies*, he declares, "I
don't really see a conflict between the church and the movies,
the sacred and the profane. . . . Both are places for people to
come together and share a common experience. I believe
there is a spirituality in films, even if it's not one which can
supplant faith."[9]

Joel and Ethan Coen. Over the years, these filmmaker brothers
have also touched on this idea of yearning and the vertical
search for meaning. Their film *O Brother Where Art Thou?*
(2000), starring George Clooney and John Turturro, was fea-
tured as an American adventure comedy and is loosely based on
Homer's epic poem "The Odyssey."

The Coens' Oscar-winning adaptation of Cormac McCarthy's
No Country for Old Men (2007) is a fascinating example of *film
noir* that's based on the Rio Grande. It is a brutally chilling
world where killers like Anton Chigurh (played by Javier

Bardem) take out innocent victims even as they plead for their lives. "You don't have to do this," we hear some of the victims plead. Yet Anton's air gun leaves a haunting mark on his victims, as well as the audience. Chigurh is evil incarnate in a godforsaken world. As sheriff Ed Tom Bell (Tommy Lee Jones) is approaching retirement, he is shocked by the dismal tide of violence that surrounds him. He opines, "The crime you see now, it's hard to even take its measure."

Alan Ball. Yet another film that has explored this theme of longing amid a bizarre world is the film *American Beauty* (1999), written by Alan Ball and starring Kevin Spacey. It was shot for 12.5 million dollars, yet grossed over three hundred million worldwide. It also took the Best Picture award, as well as Academy awards for Spacey (best actor), Sam Mendes (best director), Alan Ball (best original screenplay) and Conrad Hall (best cinematography).

American Beauty is the story of Lester Burnham, a depressed suburban father in midlife crisis, and his wife, Carolyn (played by Annette Bening), and their daughter, Jane, who are living the American dream—an idyllic, suburban, upper-middle-class life. Yet behind this rosy veneer, all is really not well. In his book *Useless Beauty: Ecclesiastes Through the Lens of Contemporary Film*, Robert K. Johnston makes this observation about the film:

> Like the artificially bred, scentless American Beauty roses that Carolyn tends in her front yard while wearing designer clogs that match her garden shears, the lives of the Burnhams are a veneer, perfect to look at on the outside but lacking any real smell or scent—any soul.[10]

While the life that is portrayed in *American Beauty* is a pristine existence—green lawns, manicured roses, designer labels and perfect smiles—there seems to be an overriding darkness, reinforced by the film's lighting and shadows, that suggests that this is no idyllic paradise. Says Alan Ball, the movie's screenwriter, "We have been led to believe that wealth and success and materialism ('stuff,' as Lester will call it) will make people happy. That is just an out-and-out lie."[11]

Paul Thomas Anderson. Like a number of young, creative filmmakers, Paul Thomas Anderson loves to mix genres and use nonlinear storytelling in his films. Many viewers are puzzled by his movies, as he regularly employs paradoxes that run through his films, yet there tends to be a latent moral imperative running in his various works.

One of Anderson's best known films is *Magnolia*, which is set on Magnolia Boulevard in Southern California's San Fernando Valley and which takes place during one twenty-four-hour period in 1999. In a frenetic succession, the film weaves the story of nine individuals. *Magnolia* truly has a strange cast of characters, portrayed by Jason Robards, Phillip Seymour Hoffman, Tom Cruise, William H. Macy and others.

In the opening montage, we hear the music overlay, "One is the loneliest number that you'll ever do," which unifies the scene. The common thread to all the characters seems to be that they are all looking for the meaning and purpose of life or at least for some semblance of happiness, given their lack of significant relationships.

While much of the film is a mélange of intersecting stories that connect only through chance and coincidence, as the film develops we begin to discover a connectedness between the vignettes that points us to a greater interconnectedness in our lives. Throughout the film, Anderson employs music as well as movies and TV to portray the possibilities and limits of wisdom. In fact, a song by the singer-songwriter Aimee Mann, "Wise Up," was Anderson's initial inspiration for the script.[12]

In reality, *Magnolia* is not a series of coincidental vignettes, but rather nine stories that play out with one unified voice, from "One is the loneliest number that you'll ever do" to "Wise Up." Even the song toward the end, "Save Me," seems to be a humble admission that no human constructs help us to figure life out. Our rationalistic assumptions about the meaning of life are tinny and hollow. We need some kind of help from above.

Perhaps Anderson's take on life, and the wisdom embedded in the film, is captured in an interview on the *Magnolia* DVD with Philip Seymour Hoffman, who has appeared in four of Anderson's movies: "The whole movie's riddled with this feeling that anything could happen at any moment. You could die or you could discover something that changes everything. So whatever you think it is you need to be doing in life, you better start doing it."[13]

Woody Allen. Another prolific and successful filmmaker, who is known for his frequent musings on faith and life, Allen has acknowledged his indebtedness to both Bergman and Scorsese as having a formidable influence on his own filmmaking. His *oeuvre* seems to perennially focus on broken relationships, the meaning of life (if there is one), God, death, morality and our sense of alienation and estrangement in this world.

Allen often raises the question "Can we really know if God exists?" Listen to the conversation between Allen's character, Boris, and Diane Keaton's character, Sonia, as Allen waxes philosophical about God's existence in the comedy *Love and Death* (1975):

Boris: Sonia, what if there is no God?

Sonia: Boris Demitrovich, are you joking?

Boris: What if we're just a bunch of absurd people who are running around with no rhyme or reason?

Sonia: But if there is no God, then life has no meaning. Why go on living? Why not just commit suicide?

Boris: Well, let's not get hysterical; I could be wrong. I'd hate to blow my brains out and then read in the papers they'd found something.

While Allen often distances himself from a Christian worldview, he nevertheless explores the dimensions of morality and guilt in his film *Crimes and Misdemeanors* (1989). The film features Martin Landau as a successful Jewish ophthalmologist who hires his brother to murder his mistress. The mistress, played by Angelica Huston, has threatened to tell his wife of their affair. The film, which mirrors Dostoevsky's classic *Crime and Punishment*, explores whether a person can commit a heinous crime and go on living as though there were no legitimacy to the guilt that results. "What Allen gives us, all in all," commented James Nuechterlein after the release of *Crimes and Misdemeanors*, "is the perspective of a man who wants to believe but cannot bring himself to do so—seemingly the prevailing plight among contemporary intellectuals."[14]

Fundamentally, Allen's worldview is one of ultimate despair. We cannot know about ultimate answers, because they do not exist. Even his Oscar-nominated *Match Point* (2005), featuring tennis pro Chris Wilton, played by Jonathan Rhys Meyers, along with his romantic interest, Nola Rice, played by Scarlett Johansson, has a subtle message about life. Life has no overarching purpose, no divine or supernatural design, and much of life is merely left to blind chance.

Allen's current views on spirituality and his agnostic take on other-worldly thinking are seen in an interview he conducted with the *New York Times* with the release of his film *You Will*

Meet a Tall Dark Stranger. Listen to the exchange between Allen and interviewer Dave Itzkoff:

Itzkoff: But there's an undercurrent, isn't there, in the new movie—not of religion, but of spirituality and supernatural phenomenon?

Allen: Well, I link them together. To me, there's no real difference between a fortune-teller or a fortune cookie and any of the organized religions. They're all equally valid or invalid, really. And equally helpful.

Itzkoff: The ideas of psychic powers and past lives, or at least people who believe in them, are central to "You Will Meet a Tall Dark Stranger." What got you interested in writing about them?

Allen: I was interested in the concept of faith in something. This sounds so bleak when I say it, but we need some delusions to keep us going. And the people who successfully delude themselves seem happier than the people who can't. I've known people who have put their faith in religion and in fortune-tellers. So it occurred to me that that was a good character for a movie: a woman who everything had failed for her, and all of a sudden, it turned out that a woman telling her fortune was helping her. The problem is, eventually, she's in for a rude awakening.

Itzkoff: What seems more plausible to you, that we've existed in past lives, or that there is a God?

Allen: Neither seems plausible to me. I have a grim, scientific assessment of it. I just feel, what you see is what you get.[15]

In Allen's perspective, humanity cannot know ultimate answers about the existence of God or an explanation for human suffering. To him, there is equal validity between fortune-telling and religion, and neither is particularly plausible in this godforsaken world of ours.

Even his most recent offering, *Midnight in Paris* (2011), starring Owen Wilson and Rachel McAdams, offers no ultimate answers. Yet it is perhaps his most winsome movie in years, reminiscent of earlier works. In *Midnight in Paris*, Allen explores the theme of nostalgia and the idea that to live in an earlier era is somehow better than our present lives.

Perhaps the best thing we can say about Allen's work is that his films and writings do show us something of the absurdity of life if there is nothing more than this temporal, blighted existence. In many ways, he serves as a modern-day Solomon, showing us the ultimate vanity of all of our chasings in life, striving after the wind.

While many of the religiously faithful may be disturbed by filmmakers such as Allen, in a post-Christian culture these artists may very well serve an important role, for they show the need for some sort of moral universe, where the violation of these truths results in legitimate guilt and estrangement, and where a life lived without facing its absurdities would be a life lived in denial.

Despite the reservations of many religious people about admitting to the reality of doubts and questionings about the apparent absurdity of life when things don't work out as planned, not all spiritually inclined people would agree. The Catholic philosopher and theologian Thomas Merton would have appreciated Allen's musings on the absurdities that we face in this temporal life. Merton wrote,

> It is only when the apparent absurdity of life is faced in all truth that faith really becomes possible. Otherwise, faith

tends to be a kind of diversion, a spiritual amusement, in which one gathers up accepted, conventional formulas and arranges them in the approved mental patterns, without bothering to investigate their meaning, or asking if they have any practical consequences in one's life.[16]

Returning to the general discussion of film as a pointer to another life, some would suggest that people are flocking to the big screen for their dose of transcendence. Modern "worshipers" who have thrown off the vestiges of traditional religious sentiments still yearn for meaning, purpose and significance.

In his novel *In the Beauty of the Lilies*, John Updike makes this very point in terms of the role of film as the contemporary means of experiencing God and getting our needs of transcendence met. This stands in marked contrast to where transcendence was encountered in an earlier era—in the church, where God would be experienced in worship. Commenting on Updike's use of cinema as the vehicle for transcendence in the novel *In the Beauty of the Lilies*, James Schiff writes,

> What makes *Lilies* such an intriguing novel is the transition Updike posits in twentieth-century American culture. Refusing to believe that God is dead, Updike suggests that God has simply become transformed, so that an individual is more likely to experience his presence in a movie theatre than in a church. . . . God's domestic light pales beside the heavenly light of the cinema. . . . With its larger than life gods and goddesses, emanating as images of light moving across and conquering the darkness, the cinema replaces the church as the dominant locus of yearning, passion, mystery, transcendence, and fulfillment. Projecting enormous images of stars who epitomize beauty and grace, the movie world stands as a heaven to which the masses aspire.[17]

In a similar vein, Geoffrey Hill, author of *Illuminating Shadows: The Mythic Power of Film*, suggests that secular "worshipers" go to the temple of the cinema for the same transcendent purposes that the Jewish people went to the religious temple.

> As ironic modern worshipers we congregate at the cinematic temple. We pay our votive offerings at the box office. We buy our ritual corn. We hush in reverent anticipation as the lights go down and the celluloid magic begins. Throughout the filmic narrative we identify with the hero. We vilify the antihero. We vicariously exult in the victories of the drama. And we are spiritually inspired by the moral of the story, all while believing we are modern techno-secular people, devoid of religion. Yet the depth and intensity of our participation reveal a religious fervor that is not much different from that of religious zealots.[18]

Ingmar Bergman. As we conclude this chapter, there is a remarkable statement worthy of reflection about the role of filmmaking from one of the great masters of modern cinema, the Swedish director Ingmar Bergman. Bergman influenced a remarkable ensemble of filmmakers who followed him. When asked about his intentions in filmmaking, his artistic vision, he said,

> The cathedral of Chartres was struck by lightning and burned to the ground. Then thousands of people came from all points of the compass, like a giant procession of ants, and together they began to rebuild the cathedral on its old site. They worked until the building was completed—master builders, artists, laborers, clowns, noblemen, priests. . . .
>   It is my opinion that art lost its basic creative drive the

moment it was separated from worship. It severed an umbilical cord and now lives its own sterile life, generating and degenerating itself. . . .

Today the individual has become the highest form and the greatest bane of artistic creation. . . . The artist considers his isolation, his subjectivity, and his individualism almost holy. Thus we finally gather in one large pen, where we stand and bleat about our loneliness without listening to each other and without realizing that we are smothering each other to death. . . . We walk in circles, so limited by our own anxieties that we can no longer distinguish between true and false . . .

I want to be one of the artists in the cathedral on the great plain. . . . Whether I believe or not, whether I am a Christian or not, I would play my part in the collective building of the cathedral.[19]

Bergman contends that in an earlier era, the artist remained unknown. He or she lived and died without being more or less "important" than other artisans, whereas today the individual, not the work of art, is exalted. To Bergman, filmmaking is a *gift*, like other artistic vocations, and should be attended not only by a sense of assurance (it is to the glory of God), but also by a natural humility. Bergman desired simply to be one of the artists in the "cathedral of the great plain." He believed that artistic expression and creative genius should not be divorced from a sense of transcendence and worship.

As we sojourn in a culture where many have become "sick of the old house of orthodoxy," to use Walker Percy's phrase, the world of literature, and especially film, provides an entrée for significant conversations about life, death, meaning and purpose.

The next time you go to the theater with friends or have someone over to watch a movie at home, think about the universal themes of life that are discussed in the movie. In what ways does the film hint of another world to come?

- 9 -

Pain and Pleasures

Touchstones of Reality

To know and to serve God, of course, is why we're here,
a clear truth that, like the nose on your face, is near at hand and
easily discernible but can make you dizzy if you try to focus on it hard.
But a little faith will see you through. What else will do except faith in
such a cynical, corrupt time? When the country goes temporarily
to the dogs, cats must learn to be circumspect, walk on
fences, sleep in trees, and have faith that all
this woofing is not the last word.

GARRISON KEILLOR

Pain insists upon being attended to.
God whispers to us in our pleasures, speaks in
our conscience, but shouts in our pains. It is
His megaphone to rouse a deaf world.

C. S. LEWIS

Pleasure is His [God's] invention,
not ours. He made the pleasures; all our research
so far has not enabled us to produce one. . . . The characteristic
of . . . pleasures is that they are unmistakably real, and
therefore, as far as they go, give the man who
feels them a touchstone of reality.

C. S. LEWIS, *THE SCREWTAPE LETTERS*

While many avenues in life serve as pointers to perhaps another reality, possibly none are so acutely felt in our experience as pain and pleasure—"touchstones of reality." While much could be said on both of these grand themes, our remarks here will be limited to how they lead to feelings of disenchantment with this present world.

The Challenge of Pain and Suffering

Confronting ultimate questions about suffering and evil is a daunting task, and we rarely have any clues as to the "why" of our painful existence. In the film *Hannah and Her Sisters*, the character played by Woody Allen tries to tell his Jewish parents that he has difficulty believing in the God of their faith. His mother won't hear of such nonsense and locks herself in the bathroom. Confused, Allen's character shouts into the bathroom, "Well, if there's a God, then why is there so much evil in the world? Just on a simplistic level, why were there Nazis?"

At this, his mother calls out from behind the bathroom door to her husband in the kitchen, "Tell him, Max."

The father replies, "How in the world do I know why there were Nazis? I don't even know how the can opener works!"

Singer Don Henley captures the heartache of a man who, as a boy, lost the love he was meant to know when his parents divorced. In the opening lines of his popular song "The End of the Innocence," he speaks of when "happily ever after fails" because "we've been poisoned by these fairy tales."

The great songwriters sing of our human losses, and we know that pain and suffering are not confined to the American scene. Worldwide tsunamis, earthquakes, revolutions, wars—we see it every day of our lives. Just turn on the television, and we quickly see that we live on a blighted planet. As you read this book, innocent blood is being shed throughout the world, tens of thousands of children are starving, many are being beaten by their parents, and millions of other people live with the squalor of disease. And the promise of a long life is a faint hope at best.

It's easy to become numbed to such tragedies, but when we experience suffering firsthand, the questions come cascading like a waterfall. The anthropologist and philosopher Loren Eiseley said that we humans are the only cosmic orphans, because only we humans ask the question "Why?"

More recently Christopher Hitchens, the best-selling author of *God Is Not Great* who found himself regularly in the media spotlight debating Christians, battled esophageal cancer until his death in 2011. His regular postings in *Vanity Fair* became quite the rage, even leading to an "Everybody Pray for Christopher Hitchens Day" on September 20, 2010. In his initial writing of his experience in *Vanity Fair*, "Topic of Cancer," an excerpt reveals this ominous event in his life:

> I have more than once in my time woken up feeling like death. But nothing prepared me for the early morning last June when I came to consciousness feeling as if I were actually shackled to my own corpse. . . . Working back from the cancer-ridden squamous cells that these first results disclosed, it took rather longer than that to discover the disagreeable truth. The word "metastasized" was the one in the report that first caught my eye, and ear. The alien had colonized a bit of my lung as well as quite a bit of my lymph node. And its original base of operations was located—had been located for quite some time—in my esophagus. My father had died, and very swiftly, too, of cancer of the esophagus. He was 79. I am 61. In whatever kind of a "race" life may be, I have very abruptly become a finalist.[1]

While Hitchens was not one to call on a deity for deliverance from his cancer, most people, even the saints, struggle with asking the Why question about human suffering. It goes without saying that it's a part of our humanness to question suffering in this life, no matter how spiritual we are.

Saint Teresa of Avila, when thrown off her carriage and deposited in a mud puddle, questioned God. He answered her, "This is how I treat all my friends." She tartly replied, "Then, Lord, it is not surprising that you have so few."[2] Even saints do not smile sweetly when God throws them into mud puddles.

After the loss of his wife to cancer, Lewis wrote of his deep grief and disillusionment with God. Published just before his death in 1963, and originally penned under the pseudonym N. W. Clerk, *A Grief Observed* asks,

> Meanwhile, where is God? . . . When you are . . . so happy that you are tempted to feel His claims upon you as an interruption, if you remember yourself and turn to Him with gratitude and praise, you will be—or so it feels—welcomed with open arms. But go to Him when your need is desperate, when all other help is vain, and what do you find? A door slammed in your face, and a sound of bolting and double bolting on the inside. . . . Why is He so present a commander in our time of prosperity and so very absent a help in time of trouble?[3]

Mark Twain observed, "When somebody you love dies, it is like when your house burns down; it isn't for years that you realize the full extent of your loss." And many of us—who, like Lewis, have lost loved ones—can greatly empathize with his startling yet candid words. We ask questions of Why, but no answers are to be found.

Yet Lewis, while admitting that God was nowhere to be found, came to realize that such muddled thinking was too superficial.

> If a good God made the world why has it gone wrong? And
> for many years I simply refused to listen to the Christian
> answers to this question. . . . My argument against God
> was that the universe seemed so cruel and unjust. But how
> had I got this idea of just and unjust? A man does not call
> a line crooked unless he has some idea of a straight line.[4]

All of us grow weary of human pain and suffering. If we did not
feel an innate sense of injustice at the atrocities, injustices and
sufferings in our mortal existence, we would be less than human.
But to question the existence of God is ultimately to question the
very standard by which we measure right and wrong.

In his book *Wishful Thinking: A Theological ABC*, Frederick
Buechner describes the dilemma of the atheist who argues
against a right and wrong:

> A true atheist is one who is willing to face the full conse-
> quences of what it means to say there is no God. To say
> there is no God means among other things that there are
> no Absolute Standards. . . . To be consistent with his creed,
> an atheist can say no more than that to beat a child to
> death is wrong with a small *w*. . . . The atheist holds the
> tabloid in his hand and asks the question Why should
> such things happen? Atheism can reply only, Why
> shouldn't such things happen? But he keeps on asking.[5]

As angry as we may become at the evil and seemingly pointless
sufferings that pervade our existence, in reality our grappling
with God is actually an indication of our righteous indignation
with this fallen world.

Consequently, with atheism, one can only state preferences
and choices, not an absolute right or wrong. In the world of

atheism, life has no ultimate meaning or purpose, and we are here only for a few short years. Embracing atheism is like screwing down the manhole covers on the great deeps and flattening the sky to a low ceiling. And instead of seeing the world as a forest of spires and turrets, like the Gothic art that expressed an age of faith, we find our world to be nothing more than a ranch-style, flattened, one-story existence.[6]

Making Some Sense Out of Suffering

Humanity loves to ask the deep questions about life and existence. We are a curious bunch. I think it was Martin Luther who, when asked what God was doing before he created the world, responded, "He was cutting up switches to flog people who ask such silly questions!" But we still want to know the answers to the tough questions of our existence, and there is nothing greater that makes us ask why than human suffering.

Unfortunately, today we live in a superficial culture that wants the bottom-line answers *right now*. Søren Kierkegaard said that religious people reminded him of schoolboys who want to look up the answers to their math problems in the back of the book rather than work them through.

T. S. Eliot once observed, "Humanity cannot stand very much reality," and rarely is this truth more obvious than when it comes to our suffering. And it's difficult for us to overcome a kind of right of entitlement, of believing that we deserve a good life, free of heartaches and pain, especially in America. But if humans are creatures who are created with higher purposes than this temporal existence, perhaps being molded and fashioned for another world that awaits us, who can imagine what measures may be used to prepare us for that magnificent destiny?

If one focuses exclusively on this temporal world's pain and death, the hope of another life set before us seems like a make-

believe story, a conjured-up fairy tale. But if one were to understand that our present trials and sufferings are preparing us for
another kind of existence, another world free of pain and suffering, it might be more palatable for us.

I am reminded of the story of the little boy who was reading
late at night before going to bed. His father noticed that his room
light was on and asked him to turn it off and go to sleep. As the
father passed his son's room, he heard his son saying softly, "If
you only knew what I knew. If you only knew what I knew." In
the morning over breakfast, the father asked his son what he
meant by the phrase. He responded, "Dad, I was really frightened
by the story I was reading. The bad guys were winning. So I
turned back to the end of the book to see how the story ended.
And you know what? The good guys won! So when I went back
to where I was in the book, every time I came to a scary part I
just repeated the phrase 'If you only knew what I knew.'"

Amid our deep grief and sorrows, to be human is to hope for
the good, for a happy ending to our sufferings in this life. Isn't it
interesting that even in our scientific age the highest-grossing
movies tend to be ones rooted in the genre of the fairy tale? We
are drawn to *happy* endings. And at a very deep level, we want
a happy ending to this human drama called life. Like much of
life, fairy tales have that intrinsic quality of struggle and pain,
and that resolution at the end that replaces pain with joy, tears
with laughter and smiles.

At the conclusion of Lewis's last installment in The Chronicles of Narnia, *The Last Battle*, Aslan reminds the Pevensie
children that, despite the pain of this world—the Shadow-
Lands—the holidays have begun.

> "Your father and mother and all of you are—as you used
> to call it in the Shadow-Lands—dead. The term is over;

the holidays have begun. The dream is ended; this is the morning." . . .

All their life in this world and all their adventures in Narnia had only been the cover and the title page; now at last they were beginning Chapter One of the Great Story, which no one on earth has read, which goes on for ever, in which every chapter is better than the one before.[7]

Pleasures and Joys: Touchstone to Another World

While pain and suffering have a way of getting our attention, and making us point to something more than this temporal existence, pleasures and joys also serve as pointers to another world.

In an earlier chapter, we looked at Solomon's vain pursuits, reminding us that no matter how much worldly success one achieves, life is still a futile chase, a wild goose chase without a goose. Blaise Pascal observed, "Anyone who does not see the vanity of life is vain indeed!"

And while we may seek pleasure and happiness through materialistic and often superficial means, one could hardly make the case that all pleasure is a bad thing. Maybe restraint should be the proper goal, but not denial. G. K. Chesterton was on to something when he observed that "the proper form of thanks for God's good gifts is some form of humility and restraint: we should thank God for beer and Burgundy by not drinking too much of them."[8]

The Origin of Pleasure

Interestingly, the origin of pleasure poses a dilemma for the atheist, just as the problem of pain does for those who embrace a Judeo-Christian worldview. As the theist must deal with the dilemma of how a good and all-powerful God could allow pain in the world, so the atheist or materialist (who denies a transcendent world to come) is under the equal obligation to explain the origin of pleasure in the world. In an atheistic world, devoid of transcendent meaning and significance, how can we account for pleasure?

Let's consider food. Why is eating so much fun? One would be hard-pressed to rival the joyful celebrations we have with family and friends centered on food. Many of us could probably write memoirs of our lives based on the fellowship and community we've experience with food as its centerpiece. It's a communal experience that heightens our sense of pleasure with those around us.

Think about the food at our weddings, funerals, anniversaries and birthdays. Obviously, we could receive our nutrition by other means, without the benefit of taste and variety, as do many of the lower animals, but it would not be nearly as delightful. On the immense joy of eating, Robert Farrar Capon observes,

> Food these days is often identified as the enemy. Butter, salt, sugar, eggs are all out to get you. And yet at our best we know better. Butter is . . . well, butter: it glorifies almost everything it touches. Salt is the sovereign of all flavors. Eggs are, pure and simple, one of the wonders of the world. And if you put them all together, you get not sudden death, but hollandaise—which in its own way is not one less bit a marvel than the Gothic arch, the computer chip, or a Bach fugue. Food, like all the other triumphs of human nature, is evidence of civilization.[9]

The pleasure that comes from the sumptuous delight in well-prepared food is beautifully portrayed in *Babette's Feast*, a film based on the play by Isak Dinesen. In the play, a French woman, Babette, enters the lives of two sisters who are members of a small ascetic religious community. After acquiring a sizable sum of money, Babette, an exile from Paris, where she served as a master chef, decides to prepare a lavish feast for them and their fellow parishioners.

Curiously, the ascetic parishioners have all taken a vow not to speak a word about the food, since they believe they should always "cleanse [their] tongues of all taste and purify them of all delight or disgust of the senses, keeping and preserving them for the higher things of praise and thanksgiving."[10]

But despite their earnest resolve, as they taste the magnificent feast that Babette has prepared for them, they cannot keep from speaking of the exquisite meal they have been privileged to experience. *Babette's Feast* reminds us that there is a transcendent aspect, something more than mere nutritional intake, that occurs when we dine on remarkably prepared food.

A few years ago, my wife and I joined friends to help celebrate their wedding anniversary. The venue was an award-winning restaurant in Napa Valley, The French Laundry, with its renowned chef and owner, Thomas Keller. Every course of the dinner was exquisitely prepared, the staff was remarkably friendly and professional, and the food and entire evening was, well, *unforgettable!*

So, how do we explain the multitude of other pleasures and joys that play such an important part in our human existence? Why is it that we have such delightful experiences from going to art shows? Or watching great cinematic films? Or listening to beautifully crafted music or being spectators of sporting events as the drama unfolds?

Do these things really contribute to our biological existence? Is there any wonder that music—such a powerful, earthly haunting—was ascribed to the gods (the muses) and not human beings? And could we not physically function just as well if we did not have movies, museums, artwork and athletic contests entertain us?

What's more, have you ever noticed how we often walk through life without any real sense of appreciation for its joys and pleasures? I came across the reflections of an anonymous Nebraskan friar who, if he had it to do over again, would do a few things differently:

> If I had my life to live over again, I'd try to make more mistakes. . . .
>
> I would relax, I would limber up, I would be sillier than I have been. . . .
>
> I know of very few things I would take seriously. I would take more trips. I would be crazier.
>
> I would climb more mountains, swim more rivers, and watch more sunsets.
>
> I would do more walking and looking. I would eat more ice cream and less beans. I would have more actual troubles, and fewer imaginary ones. . . .
>
> I'm one of those people who lives life prophylactically and sensibly hour after hour, day after day. Oh, I've had my moments, and if I had to do it over again I'd have more of them. In fact, I'd try to have nothing else, just moments, one after another, instead of living so many years ahead each day.
>
> I've been one of those people who never go anywhere without a thermometer, a hot-water bottle, a gargle, a raincoat, aspirin, and a parachute. If I had to do it over again I would go places, do things, and travel lighter. . . .
>
> I would start barefooted earlier in the spring and stay that way later in the fall. I would play hooky more. I wouldn't make such good grades, except by accident. I would ride on more merry-go-rounds. I'd pick more daisies.[11]

As we reflect on the many pleasures that are offered to us daily, we must ask ourselves, what do these pleasures tell us about this world? And what do they suggest about life?

In his book *Orthodoxy*, Chesterton deals with the origin of pleasure and how it played a significant role in his spiritual pilgrimage from atheism to a Christian worldview. Essentially, he believed that materialism was too thin a veneer to account adequately for this world of wonder and delight. In his thinking, only a romantic world infused with mystery and awe—like the story of Robinson Crusoe saving goods from his shipwreck—could account for our sense of gratitude and delight in the world. In Chesterton's thinking, the ordinary blessings of life intimate a mysterious world: "I felt in my bones; first, that this world does not explain itself. . . . There was something personal in the world, as in a work of art. . . . I thought this purpose beautiful in its old design."[12]

For Chesterton, as for us, pleasures can almost be likened to "remnants," bits of paradise washed ashore from our ancestral shipwreck. As he intimated, while the world at large may seek pleasures as the total purpose for existence, it is often the person who looks deeper, beyond this present world, to the ultimate giver as the source of these remarkable blessings.

Even Augustine, one of the greatest minds of the Christian church, was astute enough to see that pleasures are hints of another world, even of a good and generous God. Writer Philip Yancey recounts his indebtedness to Augustine on this subject of pleasures and their origin:

> I discovered in St. Augustine, a connoisseur of women, art, food, and philosophy, a guide to the goodness of created things. "The whole life of the good Christian is a holy desire," he wrote. The Latin phrase *dona bona*, or "good

gifts," appears throughout his writings. "The world is a smiling place," he insisted, and God its *largitor*, or lavisher of gifts. . . . Augustine knew well the seductions of desire that might tempt him away from the giver of good gifts. For this reason he prayed for God to gather together his "scattered longings" and keep them in their proper place.[13]

In one of his most inviting books, *Letters to Malcolm: Chiefly on Prayer*, Lewis recounted the invigorating experience of his friend turning to a brook and splashing his hot face and hands in a waterfall, no doubt reminiscent of the many hikes Lewis and his Oxford friends, the Inklings, took together.

Lewis observed that the cushiony moss, the cold water, the sound of the waterfall, along with the dancing light, while being very minor blessings compared with "the means of grace and the hope of glory," still serve as an exposition of the glory itself. These blessings are "shafts of the glory" that point to another world that awaits us:

> I was learning the far more secret doctrine that pleasures are shafts of the glory as it strikes our sensibility. . . . Gratitude exclaims, very properly, "How good of God to give me this." Adoration says, "What must be the quality of that Being whose far-off and momentary coruscations are like this!" One's mind runs back up the sunbeam to the sun. . . . Any patch of sunlight on a wood will show you something about the sun which you could never get from reading books on astronomy. These pure and spontaneous pleasures are "patches of Godlight" in the woods of our experience.[14]

So, when you and I think about our lives, which have included both terribly painful experiences (no one gets out of life without suffering) and remarkable times of delight and pleasure, what do we make of this? Don't we deep down believe that these things give purpose and meaning to life? In many ways, doesn't it make more sense to believe that they have a purpose and that they point to another world rather than to believe that they are the product of chance—the product of a random, accidental universe?

Conclusion

Is There a Remedy
for Our Disenchantment?

⁂

The human soul was made to
enjoy some object that is never fully given,
and cannot even be imagined.

C. S. LEWIS

Peter Kreeft once observed, "It is when life treats us best that the deepest dissatisfaction arises." Or, as Oscar Wilde lamented, "There are two tragedies in life. One is not getting what you want. The other is getting it."

That this present life leaves us disenchanted is a strong indication that we were made for something better: another world that awaits us. And while you and I may be unimpressed by the religious answers of our friends, can anyone really say that we aren't all searching for *something* to make sense of it all?

We have also seen how modern takes on life, explaining away the idea of God in the name of pseudo-religion, just simply don't satisfy our heart's deepest longings. A. N. Wilson, when he chronicled his return to the Christian faith after his journey in the trendy camp of unbelief, suggests why materialism *cannot* answer our deepest questions about life:

> Gilbert Ryle, with donnish absurdity, once called God "a category mistake." Yet the real category mistake made by atheists is not about God, but about human beings. Turn to the Table Talk of Samuel Taylor Coleridge—"Read the first chapter of Genesis without prejudice and you will be convinced at once. . . . 'The Lord God formed man of the dust of the ground, and breathed into his nostrils the breath of life.'"[1]

No, a brazen, materialistic take on life leaves us wanting for much more. We cannot be satisfied with such a thin veneer of an explanation. We are disenchanted in this present life, feeling a deep-down alienation with this present world, wanting so much more. Somehow it seems that we are participants in a grand drama that is unfolding before our very eyes, a "sacred drama," as Malcolm Muggeridge once observed. As physicist Freeman Dyson remarked, "The universe knew we were coming."[2]

And Solomon (the most unecclesiastical preacher we will ever encounter), in all his splendor and success, was certainly on a lifelong quest for meaning and purpose. He had acquired so many things, experienced so many pleasures of the world, and yet it left him empty, restless, disenchanted. He wanted something to satisfy his *soul*. And three thousand years later, you and I are still a lot like Solomon, though we might not want to admit it. We yearn for much more than bread and circuses.

So what's the answer to our disenchantment? Solomon realized at the end of his search that it really came back to the God question, or rather, the God solution (see Ecclesiastes 12).

But we want more than just *proof* of God's existence. Frederick Buechner writes,

We all want to be certain, we all want proof, but the kind of proof we tend to want—scientifically or philosophically demonstrable proof that would silence all doubts once and for all—would not in the long run, I think, answer the fearful depths of our need at all. For what we need to know, of course, is not just that God exists, not just that beyond the steely brightness of the stars there is a cosmic intelligence of some kind that keeps the whole show going, but that there is a God right here in the thick of our day-to-day lives who may not be writing messages about himself in the stars but who in one way or another is trying to get messages through our blindness as we move around down here knee-deep in the fragrant muck and misery and marvel of the world. It is not objective experience of God's existence that we want but, whether we use religious language for it or not, the experience of God's presence.[3]

In his book *The Question of God*, Harvard professor Armand Nicholi contrasted the two worlds of Sigmund Freud and C. S. Lewis—Freud, the renowned father of modern psychiatry and the devout atheist, and Lewis, the Oxford don turned mere Christian. While Freud dismissed religion and God as man's need for a God-figure, without any objective reality (*wishful thinking*), Lewis saw the signposts of this world in a different light (*thoughtful hoping*).

Lewis concluded that all of this world cannot be explained adequately by mere chance, but that there must be a Grand Designer behind it all. Furthermore, his writings have at their core the idea that all the attending, unfulfilled longings we experience in this life (*Sehnsucht*) serve as pointers to another world that awaits us.

One of Lewis's most memorable talks was given to students at

Oxford University in June of 1942, "The Weight of Glory." It is considered by many to be his most poignant and powerful message, in which he addresses this concept of *Sehnsucht*—"inconsolable longings"—that we experience in this present world. In Lewis's thinking, these longings speak of the glory that we may share in and that beckons us to wait in anticipation for another world to come.

> We want something else which can hardly be put into words—to be united with the beauty we see, to pass into it, to receive it into ourselves, to bathe in it, to become part of it. . . . At present we are on the outside of the world, the wrong side of the door. We discern the freshness and purity of morning, but they do not make us fresh and pure. We cannot mingle with the splendors we see. But all the leaves of the New Testament are rustling with the rumor that it will not always be so. Some day, God willing, we shall get in . . . [4]

This is the Christian hope that lies before each of us. Some day, God willing, we will have the great opportunity to enter into another world, another existence, that is unrivaled in its beauty and unspoiled nature. Wherever you are in your spiritual journey, my hope is that you would reflect deeply on your life and that you would consider the Christian message and what it says of our world, our lives and our deepest longings.

Further, my hope is that as you experience all the pleasures and joys this life has to offer, they will have their God-intended result: that they will appeal to your disenchantment, to your longing for more. As I have read and taught the writings of Lewis over the years, I have sensed a resonance with many who have come to the realization that this world just can't bring us ultimate happiness. We are, as he says in his book *The Problem of Pain*, "refreshed on the journey, but He will not allow us to mistake these temporal pleasures for home."

Furthermore, it is my hope that you will come to realize that all of the pointers in our present world—all our yearnings and longings—signify, as Augustine observed some sixteen centuries ago, that we were made for God. As Lewis wrote in one of his most powerful (though least-read) books, *Letters to Malcolm: Chiefly on Prayer,*

> We may ignore, but we can nowhere evade, the presence of God. The world is crowded with Him. He walks everywhere "incognito." And the "incognito" is not always hard to penetrate. The real labor is to remember, to attend. In fact, to come awake. Still more, to remain awake.[5]

Notes

Introduction

[1]C. S. Lewis, *Mere Christianity* (New York: HarperCollins, 2001), pp. 136-37.

Chapter 1: Looking for Answers, but Finding Only Questions

[1]John Updike, "Pigeon Feathers," in *Pigeon Feathers and Other Stories* (New York: Fawcett Columbine, 1987), pp. 135-38.

[2]Walker Percy, *Lost in the Cosmos: The Last Self-Help Book* (New York: Washington Square Press, 1983), p. 7.

[3]Daniel Boorstin, *The Image: A Guide to Pseudo-Events in America* (New York: Atheneum, 1987), p. 4.

[4]Jon Katz, *Running to the Mountain: A Journey of Faith and Change* (New York: Villard, 1999), pp. 6-7.

[5]Quoted in Peggy Noonan, "Why We Feel So Bad," *Forbes*, September 14, 1992, p. 65.

[6]Peter Kreeft, *Christianity for Modern Pagans* (San Francisco: Ignatius Press, 1993), p. 169.

[7]Walker Percy, "Novel-Writing in an Apocalyptic Time," in *Signposts in a Strange Land*, ed. Patrick Samway (New York: Farrar, Straus and Giroux, 1991), pp. 162-63.

Chapter 2: Seeking Happiness: Advice from an Ancient Sage

[1]Quoted in Peter Kreeft, *Three Philosophies of Life* (San Francisco: Ignatius Press, 1989), p. 20.

[2]Derek Kidner, *The Message of Ecclesiastes* (Downers Grove, Ill.: InterVarsity Press, 1976), p. 13.

[3]Quoted in Donald W. McCullough, *Waking from the American Dream* (Downers Grove, Ill.: InterVarsity Press, 1988), pp. 174-75.

[4]Kreeft, *Three Philosophies of Life,* p. 23.

[5]James Taylor, comments on his song "Enough to Be on Your Way," www
.sing365.com/music/lyric.nsf/Enough-To-Be-On-Your-Way-lyrics-James-
Taylor/7E6418769786D9BF482569150026D149.

Chapter 3: The Heart Has Its Reasons: The Journey of Desire

[1]Quoted in Woody Allen, "My Speech to the Graduates," New York Times,
August 10, 1979, A25.

[2]Woody Allen, "The Scrolls," in Without Feathers (New York: Random House,
1972), p. 23. The title of this book is obscure until one notices the epigram
at the beginning, which accurately reveals his cynical worldview. A line of
one of Emily Dickinson's poems says, "Hope is the thing with feathers," but
to Allen, this world is ultimately despairing, without hope.

[3]George Bernard Shaw, Too True to Be Good: A Political Extravaganza (New
York: Samuel French, 1963), n.p.

[4]Quoted in Malcolm Muggeridge, Christ and the Media (Grand Rapids:
Eerdmans, 1977), p. 62.

[5]Blaise Pascal, Pensées, trans. A. J. Krailsheimer (New York: Penguin Books,
1966), 423, 424, p. 154.

[6]Harriet Beecher Stowe, Uncle Tom's Cabin (or, Life among the Lowly), The
Minister's Wooing, Oldtown Folks (New York: Literary Classics of the United
States, 1982), pp. 352-54.

[7]Walker Percy, The Moviegoer (New York: Ballantine, 1960), pp. 9-10.

[8]Ibid., p. 25.

[9]A. N. Wilson, "Why I Believe Again," New Statesman, April 2, 2009, www
.newstatesman.com/religion/2009/04/conversion-experience-atheism.

[10]Ibid.

[11]Peter Kreeft, Heaven: The Heart's Deepest Longing (San Francisco: Ignatius
Press, 1980), p. 36.

Chapter 4: Cosmic Orphans: Our Sense of Alienation

[1]Malcolm Muggeridge, Jesus Rediscovered (New York: Doubleday, 1979), pp.
47-48.

[2]Quoted in Donald W. McCullough, Waking from the American Dream
(Downers Grove, Ill.: InterVarsity Press, 1988), pp. 199-200.

[3]Thomas Lynch, The Undertaking: Life Studies from the Dismal Trade (New
York: Norton, 1997), p. 33.

[4]Malcolm Muggeridge, Confessions of a Twentieth-Century Pilgrim (San Francisco: Harper and Row, 1988), p. 144.

[5]Peter Kreeft, Christianity for Modern Pagans (San Francisco: Ignatius Press,
1993), p. 114.

⁶Paul Johnson, *The Quest for God* (New York: HarperCollins, 1996), pp. 134-35.

⁷John Updike, *Rabbit at Rest* (New York: Ballantine, 1990), p. 16.

⁸Alan Lightman, *Einstein's Dreams* (New York: Warner, 1993), pp. 172-75.

⁹Sheldon Vanauken, *A Severe Mercy* (San Francisco: Harper and Row, 1977), p. 93.

¹⁰See Peter Kreeft, *Heaven: The Heart's Deepest Longing* (San Francisco: Ignatius Press, 1989), pp. 70-73.

¹¹Malcolm Muggeridge, *The End of Christendom* (Grand Rapids: Eerdmans, 1980), p. 16.

Chapter 5: Celebrating the Daily Humdrum

¹C. S. Lewis, *Mere Christianity* (New York: Macmillan, 1943), pp. 6-7.

²Alvaro de Silva, ed., *Brave New Family: G. K. Chesterton on Men and Women, Children, Sex, Divorce, Marriage and the Family* (San Francisco: Ignatius Press, 1990), p. 223.

³Ibid., p. 141.

⁴G. K. Chesterton, "The Home of the Unities," in *The New Witness*, January 17, 1919, cited in de Silva, p. 24.

⁵Thomas Howard, *Hallowed Be This House* (San Francisco: Ignatius Press, 1976). Many of the observations made in this chapter on the various functions of rooms in a house are derived from this excellent book.

⁶Garrison Keillor, *The Book of Guys* (New York: Viking Penguin, 1993), p. 13.

⁷Roger Shattuck, *Forbidden Knowledge* (New York: Harcourt Brace, 1996), pp. 1, 4-5.

Chapter 6: Transcendence in Our Work

¹Garrison Keillor, *The Book of Guys* (New York: Viking Penguin, 1993), pp. 11, 14.

²Michael S. Kimmel, "What Do Men Want?" *Harvard Business Review*, November-December 1993, p. 50.

³Michael S. Kimmel, *Manhood in America: A Cultural History* (New York: Free Press, 1996), p. 9.

⁴Douglas LaBier, *Modern Madness* (Reading, Mass.: Addison-Wesley, 1986), p. 25.

⁵Cited in Kimmel, "What Do Men Want?" p. 52.

⁶Leonard Woolf, as quoted in Tom L. Eisenman, *Temptations Men Face* (Downers Grove, Ill.: InterVarsity Press, 1990), p. 41.

⁷Quoted in Os Guinness, *The Call: Finding and Fulfilling the Central Purpose of Your Life* (Nashville: Word, 1998), p. 2.

⁸Dorothy L. Sayers, "Why Work?" in *Creed or Chaos?* (New York: Harcourt Brace, 1949), p. 56.

[9]C. S. Lewis, "Good Work and Good Works," in *The World's Last Night and Other Essays* (New York: Harcourt Brace Jovanovich, 1959), pp. 71, 80.

[10]Tom Morris, *If Aristotle Ran General Motors* (New York: Henry Holt, 1997), pp. xiii-xiv.

[11]Cited in ibid., p. 17.

[12]Frederick Buechner, "Vocation," in *Wishful Thinking: A Theological ABC* (New York: Harper and Row, 1973), p. 95.

Chapter 7: Leisure and Play: Looking for Paradise?

[1]Josef Pieper, "Leisure and Its Threefold Opposition," in *Josef Pieper: An Anthology* (San Francisco: Ignatius Press, 1989), p. 140.

[2]M. Scott Peck, *Golf and the Spirit: Lessons for the Journey* (New York: Harmony Books, 1999), p. 3.

[3]John Feinstein, *A Good Walk Spoiled: Days and Nights on the PGA Tour* (Boston: Little, Brown, 1995), pp. xvi-xvii.

[4]Cited in ibid., p. xvii.

[5]Jay Tolson, *Pilgrim in the Ruins: A Life of Walker Percy* (New York: Simon and Schuster, 1992), p. 27.

[6]John Updike, "Moral Exercise," in *Golf Dreams: Writings on Golf* (New York: Knopf, 1996), pp. 44-45.

[7]Michael Murphy, *Golf in the Kingdom* (New York: Penguin Arkana, 1972), pp. 164-66. *Hamartiology* comes from the Greek word *hamartia* and carries with it the idea of someone "missing the mark," or in Christian theology, "missing the mark of perfection."

[8]Peck, *Golf and the Spirit*, pp. 4-5.

[9]John Updike, "Moral Exercise," p. 44.

[10]George F. Will, *Men at Work: The Craft of Baseball* (New York: Harper Perennial, 1991), p. 2.

[11]Thomas Boswell, *Why Time Begins on Opening Day* (New York: Penguin, 1984), p. 288.

[12]A. Bartlett Giamatti, "Baseball and the American Character," in *A Great and Glorious Game: Baseball Writings of A. Bartlett Giamatti*, ed. Kenneth S. Robson (Chapel Hill, N.C.: Algonquin Books of Chapel Hill, 1998), pp. 64-65.

Chapter 8: Transcendence in Literature and Film

[1]See Peter Kreeft, *Heaven: The Heart's Deepest Longing* (San Francisco: Ignatius Press, 1989), pp. 110-11.

[2]Cited in Timothy Keller, *The Reason for God: Belief in an Age of Skepticism* (New York: Dutton, 2008), p. 133.

[3]*John Updike and Religion: The Sense of the Sacred and the Motions of Grace*, ed. James Yerkes (Grand Rapids: Eerdmans, 1999), pp. 3-4.

[4]Reynolds Price, "At the Heart," in *A Common Room: Essays 1954-1987* (New York: Atheneum, 1989), p. 405.

[5]C. S. Lewis, "On Three Ways of Writing for Children," in *Of Other Worlds: Essays and Stories* (New York: Harcourt Brace, 1966), pp. 29-30.

[6]J. R. R. Tolkien, "On Fairy Stories," in *A Tolkien Reader* (New York: Ballantine, 1966), p. 37.

[7]*The Departed*, written by William Monohan, directed by Martin Scorsese, DVD (Warner Home Video, 2006).

[8]Quoted in Bob Minzesheimer, "Mixing Movies and Mysticism," *USA Today*, January 12, 1998, D1.

[9]Ibid.

[10]Robert K. Johnston, *Useless Beauty: Ecclesiastes through the Lens of Contemporary Film* (Grand Rapids: Baker Academic, 2004), p. 58.

[11]Ibid., pp. 59-60.

[12]Ibid., p. 80.

[13]Ibid., p. 91.

[14]James Nuechterlein, "Godless and Guiltless, a Disorderly Cosmos," *New York Times*, October 15, 1989, H15f.

[15]Dave Itzkoff, "Woody Allen: The Director's Cut," ArtsBeat: The Culture at Large, *New York Times*, September 15, 2010, http://artsbeat.blogs.nytimes.com/2010/09/15/woody-allen-the-directors-cut/.

[16]Thomas Merton, *Disputed Questions* (New York: Farrar, Straus and Giroux, 1960), p. 166.

[17]James A. Schiff, "The Pocket Nothing Else Will Fill: Updike's Domestic God," in *John Updike and Religion: The Sense of the Sacred and the Motions of Grace* (Grand Rapids: Eerdmans, 1999), pp. 61-62.

[18]Geoffrey Hill, *Illuminating Shadows: The Mythic Power of Film* (Boston: Shambhala, 1992), p. 3.

[19]Ingmar Bergman, *Four Screenplays of Ingmar Bergman* (New York: Simon and Schuster, 1960), from the introduction.

Chapter 9: Pain and Pleasures: Touchstones of Reality

[1]Christopher Hitchens, "Topic of Cancer," *Vanity Fair*, September 2010, www.davidabrahamson.com/www/ialjs/hitchens_topicofcancer_vanityfair_sept2010.pdf.

[2]Cited in Peter Kreeft, *Making Sense Out of Suffering* (Ann Arbor, Mich.: Servant Books, 1986), p. 15.

[3]C. S. Lewis, *A Grief Observed* (New York: Seabury Press, 1961), p. 9.

[4]C. S. Lewis, *Mere Christianity* (New York: Macmillan, 1942), p. 31. Lewis made a similar admission in *The Problem of Pain* (New York: Touchstone, 1996) when he observed, "If the universe is so bad, or even half so bad, how on earth did human beings ever come to attribute it to the activity of a wise and good Creator? Men are fools, perhaps; but hardly so foolish as that" (p. 13).

[5]Frederick Buechner, "Atheist," in *Wishful Thinking: A Theological ABC* (New York: Harper and Row, 1973), pp. 2-4.

[6]See Kreeft, *Making Sense*, p. 32.

[7]C. S. Lewis, *The Last Battle* (New York: Macmillan, 1956), pp. 183-84.

[8]G. K. Chesterton, *Orthodoxy* (San Francisco: Ignatius Press, 1995), p. 70.

[9]Robert Farrar Capon, *The Supper of the Lamb—A Culinary Reflection* (New York: Farrar, Straus and Giroux, 1989), p. xiii.

[10]Isak Dinesen, *Babette's Feast and Other Anecdotes of Destiny* (New York: Vintage Books, 1988), p. 27.

[11]Cited in Tim Hansel, *When I Relax I Feel Guilty* (Elgin, Ill.: David C. Cook, 1979), pp. 44-45.

[12]Chesterton, *Orthodoxy*, pp. 69-70.

[13]Philip Yancey, *Rumors of Another World* (Grand Rapids: Zondervan, 2003), pp. 36-37.

[14]C. S. Lewis, *Letters to Malcolm: Chiefly on Prayer* (New York: Harcourt Brace Jovanovich, 1963), pp. 89-91.

Conclusion: Is There a Remedy for Our Disenchantment?

[1]A. N. Wilson, "Why I Believe Again," *The New Statesman*, April 2, 2009, www.newstatesman.com/religion/2009/04/conversion-experience-atheism.

[2]Freeman Dyson, quoted in Karl W. Giberson, "The Goldilocks Universe," *Books and Culture*, January-February 2003, p. 30.

[3]Frederick Buechner, "Message in the Stars," in *Secrets in the Dark: A Life of Sermons* (San Francisco: Harper SanFrancisco, 2006), pp. 18-19.

[4]C. S. Lewis, *The Weight of Glory: and Other Addresses* (New York: Harper-Collins, 2001), pp. 42-44.

[5]C. S. Lewis, *Letters to Malcolm: Chiefly on Prayer* (New York: Harcourt Brace Jovanovich, 1963), p. 75.

About the Author

Barry Morrow brings over twenty-five years of experience in working in the marketplace with businessmen through teaching, speaking and consulting, primarily through his organization, FinishingWell (Finishingwell.com).

Initially pursuing a career in medicine, Barry received an undergraduate degree in biology from the University of North Carolina at Chapel Hill. After working in business for a few years, he attended Dallas Theological Seminary where he graduated with high honors. At Dallas Seminary he received a master's degree in semitics and Old Testament studies; he was awarded the Jennie Solomon Award in Old Testament.

Barry enjoys movies, reading and golf, and he is passionate about baseball. Occasionally, when he can make his way to Oxford, England, he can be found exploring the haunts of C. S. Lewis and his Inklings companions at the Eagle and Child Pub (affectionately known as the Bird and the Baby) on St. Giles.

Follow Barry on Facebook at barrymorrow, and Twitter at twitter.com/barrymorrow.